100
French Dishes

100
French Dishes

Edited by
Rhona Newman

octopus

Contents

NOTES
Standard spoon measurements are used in all recipes
1 tablespoon = one 15 ml spoon
1 teaspoon = one 5 ml spoon
All spoon measures are level.

Fresh herbs are used unless otherwise stated. If unobtainable, substitute a bouquet garni of the equivalent dried herbs, or use dried herbs instead but halve the quantities stated.
Ovens and grills (broilers) should be preheated to the specified temperature or heat setting.
For all recipes, quantities are given in metric, imperial and American measures. Follow one set of measures only, because they are not interchangeable.

First published 1983 by
Octopus Books Limited
59 Grosvenor Street, London W1

© 1983 Octopus Books Limited

ISBN 0 7064 1928 6

Produced by Mandarin Publishers Ltd
22a Westlands Rd
Quarry Bay, Hong Kong

Printed in Hong Kong

Frontispiece: Gascony Turkey (page 30)
(Photograph: British Turkey Federation)

Introduction

Meals have more of a sense of occasion in France than in other countries. The time and effort spent by a French housewife will always be appreciated by her family and guests. Breakfast is a light meal – usually hot coffee or chocolate with a roll or croissant. The main meal is often eaten at lunchtime as most shops and offices have a two hour break for lunch. This meal may be simple soup or starter such as a light egg or vegetable dish, followed by the meat or fish course. The vegetable dishes are served separately, often followed by a tossed green salad. The cheese is served before the dessert and the meal is rounded off with black coffee. Wine is always served with a meal.

The recipes in this book aim to give a selection of classic and regional French dishes which are frequently served in homes and restaurants. For easy reference, the recipes have been divided into the following chapters.

Soups and Pâtés

"Potage" or soup is the mainstay of simple French cooking. Many homes and restaurants have a pot continually simmering on the stove. Soups vary from thin consommés to the rich-flavoured fish soups such as bouillabaisse. Serve soups with warm crusty French bread or fried croûtons.

France is justly famous for its pâtés and terrines which can be a rich delicacy or a basic everyday dish. They are made from a mixture of meats such as pork, bacon and offal (variety meats), flavoured with herbs, garlic, onion and wine then bound with eggs. The texture of the pâté can be coarse like Pâté de Campagne or smooth like Chicken Liver Pâté.

Fish Dishes

There are many varieties of fish and shellfish caught around the coast of France which has led to local dishes becoming specialities. Open markets are the place to find the freshly caught familiar and the not-so-familiar fish. French fish dishes can be whole fish served simply, fillets stuffed or rolled and coated in a sauce or the Mediterranean style stews which include garlic, wine and tomatoes. Traditional shellfish dishes include Coquilles St Jacques and Moules Marinière.

Meat and Poultry Dishes

Good butchering is an art in France, the method of cutting meat being quite different from that in Britain and America. French meat dishes are either good cuts of meat served simply, or the cheaper cuts which require long, slow cooking. Many of the latter are regional or traditional dishes which are always well flavoured and often include wine.

Many good poultry dishes are made in France, the method of cooking and the flavouring depending on the age of the bird.

Egg and Cheese Dishes

The French are said to have several hundred ways of cooking eggs, perhaps the most famous are omelettes, soufflés, crêpes and quiches. Eggs are popular served as a first course, as a light meal or in custards, ices and sweet flans for dessert.

France is well known for its great variety of cheeses – different flavours, textures, sizes and shapes of cheeses abound. Many are now produced on a commercial basis and exported, but others are still made locally on farms.

Salads and Vegetable Dishes

Quality is particularly important to the French when choosing fruit and vegetables. Vegetables are rarely just boiled as this results in loss of flavour, colour and nutrients. Some of the recipes included here can be served after the meat or fish course. Other dishes like stuffed vegetables, Layered Aubergine (Eggplant) and Carrot Terrine or Pissaladière are more suitable to serve as appetizers or light meals.

Salads also rely on good fresh ingredients. A green salad consisting of lettuce and possibly watercress or young dandelion leaves tossed in oil and vinegar will be served at least once a day in a French home. A Salad Niçoise is more likely to be served as a starter.

Gâteaux and Desserts

These are reserved for special occasions as many are rather rich and extravagant. For an everyday meal, it is more usual for the French to serve fresh fruit or yogurt after the cheese course.

Pastry shops are a great attraction in France where you can buy light sponges, gâteaux, meringues, fruit flans and confections of puff or choux pastry, as well as several varieties of rich yeast dough. In many French cities, afternoon tea has become fashionable and these confections may be served with lemon tea or coffee as well as for dessert.

The recipes in this book provide a delicious taste of France – *bon appétit!*

5

Soups & Pâtés

Bouillabaisse

METRIC/IMPERIAL	AMERICAN
2 tablespoons oil	2 tablespoons oil
1 large onion, sliced	1 large onion, sliced
1 clove garlic, crushed	1 clove garlic, crushed
2 × 397 g/14 oz cans tomatoes	2 × 16 oz cans tomatoes
300 ml/½ pint fish stock	1¼ cups fish stock
2 tablespoons chopped parsley	2 tablespoons chopped parsley
salt and pepper	salt and pepper
1 bouquet garni	1 bouquet garni
450 g/1 lb monkfish, diced	1 lb monkfish, diced
1 × 675 g/1½ lb red fish, skinned and filleted	1 × 1½ lb red fish, skinned and filleted
350 g/12 oz coley fillet, skinned and diced	¾ lb coley fillet, skinned and diced
350 g/12 oz catfish fillet, skinned and diced	¾ lb catfish, skinned and diced
4 × 175 g/6 oz plaice fillets, skinned and cut into strips	4 × 6 oz flounder fillets, skinned and cut into strips
parsley to garnish	parsley for garnish

Heat the oil in a large pan and sauté the onion and garlic for 5 minutes. Add the tomatoes with their juice, stock, parsley, salt and pepper to taste and bouquet garni. Bring to the boil, then simmer for 10 minutes.

Add the monkfish and red fish and cook for 5 minutes. Stir in the coley and catfish and simmer for a further 5 minutes.

Finally add the plaice (flounder) and simmer for 5 to 10 minutes or until all the fish is cooked. Remove the bouquet garni and adjust the seasoning. Pour the soup into a tureen and sprinkle with parsley. Serve with hot French bread.
Cooking time: 30 to 40 minutes
Serves 8
Note: any fish can be used to make bouillabaisse but it is important to cook the firmer fish first, then to add the more flaky ones. Shellfish, such as prawns (shrimp), lobster pieces, mussels or clams can be added to the soup as well.

Bouillabaisse
(Photograph: Sea Fish Kitchen)

French Onion Soup

METRIC/IMPERIAL	AMERICAN
40 g/1½ oz butter	3 tablespoons butter
350 g/12 oz onions, sliced	3 cups sliced onion
900 ml/1½ pints beef stock	3¾ cups beef stock
1 tablespoon dry sherry	1 tablespoon dry sherry
salt and pepper	salt and pepper
4 slices French bread	4 slices French bread
50 g/2 oz Cheddar cheese, grated	½ cup grated Cheddar cheese

Melt the butter in a pan and sauté the onions for 5 minutes. Add the stock and bring to the boil, then stir in the sherry and salt and pepper to taste. Cover the pan and simmer the soup for 45 minutes.

Pour the soup into 4 heatproof bowls and float the bread on top. Sprinkle with the cheese and place under a preheated grill (broiler) to brown. Serve immediately.
Cooking time: 55 minutes
Serves 4

Continental Potage

METRIC/IMPERIAL
2 tablespoons
  vegetable oil
1 onion, sliced
225 g/8 oz potatoes,
  peeled and diced
2 carrots, sliced
2 sticks celery,
  chopped
1 × 397 g/14 oz can
  tomatoes
600 ml/1 pint beef
  stock
1 bay leaf
grated nutmeg
salt and pepper
100 g/4 oz smoked
  sausage, chopped
75 g/3 oz white
  cabbage, shredded
chopped parsley to
  garnish

AMERICAN
2 tablespoons
  vegetable oil
1 onion, sliced
1⅓ cups diced potato
2 carrots, sliced
2 stalks celery, sliced
1 × 16 oz can
  tomatoes
2½ cups beef stock
1 bay leaf
grated nutmeg
salt and pepper
½ cup chopped
  smoked sausage
1 cup shredded white
  cabbage
chopped parsley for
  garnish

Heat the oil in a large pan and sauté the onion, potatoes, carrots and celery for 5 minutes.

Add the tomatoes with their juice, stock, bay leaf, nutmeg and salt and pepper to taste. Bring to the boil, cover and simmer for 20 minutes.

Add the smoked sausage and cabbage and continue to cook for 15 to 20 minutes. Adjust the seasoning and pour into warm soup bowls. Garnish with parsley.
Cooking time: 45 minutes
Serves 4 to 6

Mint Pea Soup

METRIC/IMPERIAL
350 g/12 oz potatoes,
  peeled and
  chopped
salt and pepper
300 ml/½ pint boiling
  water
3 to 4 sprigs fresh
  mint
2 spring onions,
  chopped
300 g/10 oz cooked
  peas
1 teaspoon lemon
  juice
150 ml/¼ pint single
  cream
fresh mint to garnish

AMERICAN
¾ lb potatoes, peeled
  and chopped
salt and pepper
1¼ cups boiling
  water
3 to 4 sprigs fresh
  mint
2 scallions, chopped
1¾ cups cooked peas
1 teaspoon lemon
  juice
⅔ cup light cream
fresh mint for garnish

Place the potatoes in a pan and cover with cold water. Add salt and bring to the boil. Cover and simmer for 20 minutes, then drain, reserving 150 ml/¼ pint (⅔ cup) of the liquid.

Pour the boiling water over the mint and spring onions (scallions) and leave to infuse for 15 minutes.

Place the potatoes, reserved liquid, infused liquid with the mint and onions (scallions), peas, lemon juice and salt and pepper to taste in a blender or food processor. Work to a purée and pour into a pan. Stir in the cream and heat through gently. Adjust the seasoning. Serve hot or cold garnished with mint.
Cooking time: 30 minutes
Serves 4 to 6

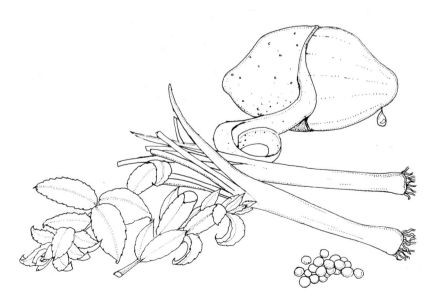

Potage Parmentier

METRIC/IMPERIAL	AMERICAN
225 g/8 oz potatoes	½ lb potatoes
25 g/1 oz margarine	2 tablespoons margarine
1 onion, sliced	1 onion, sliced
40 g/1½ oz plain flour	6 tablespoons all-purpose flour
1.2 litres/2 pints water	5 cups water
salt and pepper	salt and pepper
150 ml/¼ pint milk	⅔ cup milk
croûtons to serve	croûtons to serve

Peel and slice the potatoes and leave to stand in cold water.

Melt the margarine in a pan and sauté the onion until soft. Stir in the flour and cook for 1 minute. Remove from the heat and gradually blend in the water. Add the potatoes and salt and pepper to taste. Bring to the boil and simmer for 45 minutes to 1 hour. Allow to cool slightly then place in a blender or food processor or pass through a sieve to make a purée.

Return the soup to the pan and add the milk. Adjust the seasoning and heat through gently. Pour into warm soup bowls and serve with croûtons.
Cooking time: 1 to 1¼ hours
Serves 4 to 6

Provençal Vegetable Soup

METRIC/IMPERIAL	AMERICAN
2 carrots, diced	2 carrots, diced
2 green peppers, cored, seeded and diced	2 green peppers, seeded and diced
2 onions, sliced	2 onions, sliced
2 leeks, sliced	2 leeks, sliced
2 sticks celery, chopped	2 stalks celery, chopped
225 g/8 oz tomatoes, skinned	½ lb tomatoes, peeled
1 clove garlic, crushed	1 clove garlic, crushed
750 ml/1¼ pints beef stock	3 cups beef stock
150 ml/¼ pint red wine	⅔ cup red wine
1 teaspoon mixed herbs	1 teaspoon mixed herbs
1 bay leaf	1 bay leaf
salt and pepper	salt and pepper

In a large pan place the carrots, peppers, onions, leeks, celery, tomatoes and garlic.

Pour over the stock and wine, then add the herbs, bay leaf and salt and pepper to taste.

Bring to the boil, cover and simmer for 1½ hours. Adjust the seasoning, remove the bay leaf and serve in warm soup bowls with chunks of crusty bread.
Cooking time: 1½ hours
Serves 4 to 6

Vichyssoise

METRIC/IMPERIAL	AMERICAN
25 g/1 oz butter	2 tablespoons butter
1 leek, sliced	1 leek, sliced
1 small onion, sliced	1 small onion, sliced
750 ml/1¼ pints chicken stock	3 cups chicken stock or broth
350 g/12 oz potatoes, peeled and sliced	¾ lb potatoes, peeled and sliced
1 bouquet garni	1 bouquet garni
salt and pepper	salt and pepper
150 ml/¼ pint single cream	⅔ cup light cream
chopped chives to garnish	chopped chives for garnish

Melt the butter in a pan and sauté the leek and onion until soft. Add the stock, potatoes, bouquet garni and salt and pepper to taste. Bring to the boil, then cover and simmer for 20 to 30 minutes or until the potatoes are soft.

Remove the bouquet garni, allow the soup to cool slightly, then place in a blender or food processor or pass through a sieve to make a purée.

Return to the pan, add the cream and heat through gently. Adjust the seasoning and pour into warm soup bowls. Garnish with chives.
Cooking time: 35 to 45 minutes
Serves 4

Pâté de Campagne

METRIC/IMPERIAL	AMERICAN
225 g/8 oz veal, minced	½ lb boneless veal for stew, ground
225 g/8 oz belly pork, minced	½ lb fresh pork sides, ground
225 g/8 oz pigs' liver, minced	½ lb pork liver, ground
225 g/8 oz sausagemeat	1 cup pork sausage meat
1 clove garlic, crushed	1 clove garlic, crushed
1 teaspoon mustard powder	1 teaspoon mustard powder
6 allspice berries, crushed	6 allspice berries, crushed
2 tablespoons brandy	2 tablespoons brandy
salt and pepper	salt and pepper
100 g/4 oz streaky bacon	¼ lb fatty bacon slices
2 bay leaves	2 bay leaves

Place the veal, pork, liver and sausagemeat in a bowl and mix well. Blend in the garlic, mustard, allspice, brandy and salt and pepper to taste.

Spoon the mixture into a greased 900 ml/1½ pint (5 cup) terrine or soufflé dish and smooth over the top. Lay the bacon and bay leaves over the top. Cover with foil and place in a roasting pan. Add water to come 2.5 cm/1 inch up the dish. Cook in a preheated moderate oven (160°C/325°F, Gas Mark 3) for 1½ hours. Cool and chill before serving.
Cooking time: 1½ hours
Serves 6

Chicken Liver Pâté

METRIC/IMPERIAL	AMERICAN
450 g/1 lb chicken livers	1 lb chicken livers
1 onion, chopped	1 onion, chopped
175 g/6 oz butter	¾ cup butter
2 teaspoons mustard powder	2 teaspoons mustard powder
1 teaspoon dried mixed herbs	1 teaspoon dried mixed herbs
1 teaspoon salt	1 teaspoon salt
½ teaspoon freshly ground pepper	½ teaspoon freshly ground pepper
1 radish to garnish	1 radish for garnish

Place the chicken livers and onion in a pan with 50 g/2 oz (¼ cup) butter. Cook gently until livers are not pink inside and onion is soft.

Remove from the heat and blend the livers and onion in a blender or food processor, or rub through a sieve until smooth. Add the remaining butter, mustard, mixed herbs, salt and pepper. Mix well then turn into a serving dish. Chill. Garnish with the radish.
Cooking time: 10 minutes
Serves 4

Devilled Potted Chicken

METRIC/IMPERIAL	AMERICAN
225 g/8 oz cooked chicken	½ lb cooked chicken
100 g/4 oz butter	½ cup butter
2 teaspoons mustard powder	2 teaspoons mustard powder
2 teaspoons Worcestershire sauce	2 teaspoons Worcestershire sauce
salt and pepper	salt and pepper
lemon slices and watercress to garnish	lemon slices and watercress for garnish

Mince the chicken meat or blend in a blender or food processor. Gradually mix in the butter, mustard, Worcestershire sauce and salt and pepper to taste.

Press the mixture into 4 dishes or a 450 ml/¾ pint (2 cup) soufflé dish. Chill and serve garnished with lemon slices and watercress.
Serves 4

Clockwise from back: Smoked Mackerel Pâté (page 12); Chicken Liver Pâté; Devilled Potted Chicken; Pâté de Campagne
(Photograph: Colman's Mustard)

Smoked Mackerel Pâté

METRIC/IMPERIAL	AMERICAN
4 smoked mackerel fillets, skinned and boned	4 smoked mackerel fillets, skinned and boned
1 teaspoon mustard powder	1 teaspoon mustard powder
50 g/2 oz butter	¼ cup butter
40 g/1½ oz plain flour	6 tablespoons all-purpose flour
300 ml/½ pint milk	1¼ cups milk
15 g/½ oz gelatine	2 tablespoons unflavored gelatin
2 tablespoons lemon juice	2 tablespoons lemon juice
300 ml/½ pint double cream	1¼ cups heavy cream
salt and pepper	salt and pepper

Pound the mackerel until smooth or blend in a blender or food processor, then mix in the mustard.

Melt the butter in a pan, add the flour and cook for 1 minute. Remove from the heat and gradually stir in the milk. Return to the heat and stir the sauce until it thickens. Allow to cool.

Sprinkle the gelatine over the lemon juice in a heatproof bowl and stand in a pan of gently simmering water. Stir until the gelatine dissolves.

In a bowl, mix together the fish, sauce and gelatine. Whip the cream until thick and fold into the fish mixture. Add salt and pepper to taste.

Pour into a 900 ml/1½ pint (5 cup) mould or soufflé dish. Place in the refrigerator until set then invert onto a serving platter. Serve with hot toast fingers and a salad.

Cooking time: 10 minutes
Serves 6 to 8
Illustrated on page 11

Pâté Maison

METRIC/IMPERIAL	AMERICAN
100 g/4 oz lean bacon	¼ lb lean bacon slices
3 tablespoons brandy	3 tablespoons brandy
450 g/1 lb calves' liver, minced	1 lb calf liver, ground
100 g/4 oz belly pork, minced	¼ lb fresh pork sides, ground
1 egg	1 egg
2 tablespoons double cream	2 tablespoons heavy cream
2 tablespoons lemon juice	2 tablespoons lemon juice
1 clove garlic, crushed	1 clove garlic, crushed
salt and pepper	salt and pepper
50 g/2 oz chicken livers, coarsely chopped	¼ cup coarsely chopped chicken livers

Remove the rind from the bacon, then use the bacon to line a 600 ml/1 pint (2½ cup) ovenproof dish. Spoon over the brandy.

Mix together the calves' liver, pork, egg, cream, lemon juice, garlic and salt and pepper to taste. Place half the mixture in the bacon lined dish. Add the chicken livers, then top with the remaining meat mixture.

Stand the dish in a roasting pan and add water to come 2.5 cm/1 inch up the sides. Cook in a preheated cool oven (150°C/300°F, Gas Mark 2) for 2 hours. If the pâté becomes too brown, cover it with foil.

Remove the pâté from the oven and place a weight on top. Chill in the refrigerator overnight. Invert onto a serving platter and serve with fingers of hot toast.

Cooking time: 2 hours
Serves 6

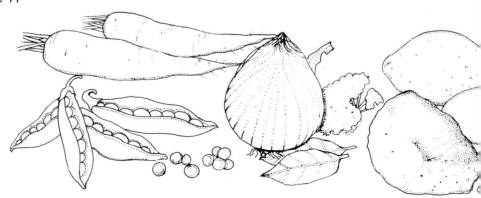

French Country-Style Pâté

METRIC/IMPERIAL	AMERICAN
175 g/6 oz pigs' liver, sliced	6 oz pork liver, sliced
100 g/4 oz lean bacon	¼ lb lean bacon slices
100 g/4 oz stewing veal	¼ lb boneless veal for stew
1 small onion, chopped	1 small onion, chopped
2 cloves garlic, crushed	2 cloves garlic, crushed
50 g/2 oz fresh white breadcrumbs	1 cup soft white bread crumbs
1 tablespoon chopped parsley	1 tablespoon chopped parsley
2 eggs, beaten	2 eggs, beaten
150 ml/¼ pint milk	⅔ cup milk
salt and pepper	salt and pepper
3 bay leaves	3 bay leaves

Cover the liver with boiling water and leave for 5 minutes. Drain and mince (grind) the liver with the bacon, veal and onion.

Add the garlic, breadcrumbs, parsley, eggs, milk and salt and pepper to taste. Mix well and spoon into a greased 500 g/1 lb loaf tin (7 × 3 inch loaf pan). Place the bay leaves on top and cover with foil.

Cook in a preheated moderate oven (160°C/325°F, Gas Mark 3) for 1 hour. Leave in the tin (pan) for 5 minutes. Remove the bay leaves and invert the pâté onto a serving platter. Chill and serve cut into slices.
Cooking time: 1 hour
Serves 4

Chicken and Vegetable Terrine

METRIC/IMPERIAL	AMERICAN
225 g/8 oz raw chicken meat	½ lb raw chicken meat
150 ml/¼ pint double cream	⅔ cup heavy cream
salt and pepper	salt and pepper
2 teaspoons chopped parsley	2 teaspoons chopped parsley
2 carrots, peeled	2 carrots, peeled
75 g/3 oz French beans	⅓ cup green beans
75 g/3 oz peas	½ cup peas

Mince the chicken meat twice or put through a food processor. Mix the chicken with the cream, salt and pepper to taste and parsley.

Cut the carrots into matchsticks. Blanch the carrots, beans and peas in boiling salted water in three separate pans for 2 minutes. Drain thoroughly.

Arrange a few carrot sticks and peas in the base of a greased 600 ml/1 pint (2½ cup) ovenproof dish. Spread with a layer of chicken. Continue layering the peas, chicken, beans and carrots. Cover with buttered greaseproof (waxed) paper and foil.

Place the dish in a roasting pan half filled with boiling water. Cook in a preheated moderate oven (160°C/325°F, Gas Mark 3) for 45 minutes to 1 hour or until the terrine is firm to touch.

Leave to cool then drain off any excess liquid. Invert onto a serving platter and chill thoroughly. Serve with mayonnaise and bread and butter.
Cooking time: 45 minutes to 1 hour
Serves 4

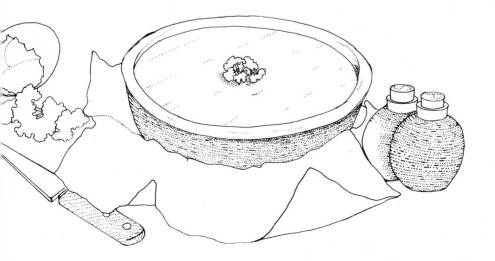

Fish Dishes

Cod with French Mustard Sauce

METRIC/IMPERIAL	AMERICAN
2 tablespoons plain flour	2 tablespoons all-purpose flour
salt and pepper	salt and pepper
4 cod steaks	4 cod steaks
40 g/1½ oz butter	3 tablespoons butter
Sauce:	**Sauce:**
40 g/1½ oz butter	3 tablespoons butter
40 g/1½ oz plain flour	6 tablespoons all-purpose flour
300 ml/½ pint milk	1¼ cups milk
3 teaspoons French mustard	3 teaspoons Dijon-style mustard
1 tablespoon chopped parsley	1 tablespoon chopped parsley
salt and pepper	salt and pepper
parsley sprigs to garnish	parsley sprigs for garnish

Season the flour with salt and pepper and use to coat the cod steaks. Place the fish in the bottom of the grill (broiler) pan. Dot with the butter and grill (broil) for 8 minutes on each side, or until the fish is white and tender.

To make the sauce: melt the butter in a pan and stir in the flour. Cook for 1 minute, then remove from the heat. Gradually blend in the milk. Return the sauce to the heat and cook, stirring, until the sauce thickens. Add the mustard, parsley and salt and pepper to taste.

Arrange the cod steaks on a warm serving platter and pour the sauce over. Garnish with parsley.
Cooking time: 30 minutes
Serves 4

Trout with Duck Pâté and Orange Stuffing

METRIC/IMPERIAL	AMERICAN
grated rind and juice of 2 oranges	grated rind and juice of 2 oranges
1 small onion, finely chopped	1 small onion, finely chopped
100 g/4 oz duck pâté	¼ lb duck pâté
100 g/4 oz fresh brown breadcrumbs	2 cups soft brown bread crumbs
1 tablespoon chopped parsley	1 tablespoon chopped parsley
40 g/1½ oz walnuts, chopped	⅓ cup chopped walnuts
salt and pepper	salt and pepper
4 trout	4 trout
Garnish:	**Garnish:**
orange slices	orange slices
walnut halves	walnut halves

In a bowl, mix together the orange rind, juice, onion, pâté, breadcrumbs, parsley, walnuts and salt and pepper to taste.

Wash, clean and trim the trout, then use the stuffing to fill the cavities. Fold the trout over and arrange in a greased, shallow ovenproof dish. Cover with foil and cook in a preheated moderate oven (160°C/325°F, Gas Mark 3) for 30 to 35 minutes.

Carefully remove the fish and place on a warm serving platter. Garnish with orange slices and walnut halves.
Cooking time: 30 to 35 minutes
Serves 4

Cod with French Mustard Sauce
(Photograph: Colman's Mustard)

Coquilles St. Jacques Patricia

METRIC/IMPERIAL	AMERICAN
4 × 3.5 cm/1½ inch slices white bread	4 × 1½ inch slices white bread
100 g/4 oz butter	½ cup butter
1 small onion, finely chopped	1 small onion, finely chopped
150 ml/¼ pint dry white wine	⅔ cup dry white wine
150 ml/¼ pint double cream	⅔ cup heavy cream
8 large scallops, opened	8 large scallops, shucked
2 eggs, separated	2 eggs, separated
salt and pepper	salt and pepper
2 tablespoons grated Parmesan cheese	2 tablespoons grated Parmesan cheese
Garnish:	**Garnish:**
cayenne pepper	cayenne
watercress	watercress

Using a 10 cm/4 inch plain cutter, cut circles out of the bread slices. Using a 7.5 cm/3 inch plain cutter, carefully remove the centres from the rounds to make 4 hollow croustades with bases and thin walls.

Melt 75 g/3 oz (⅓ cup) butter and use to brush the croustades. Place on a baking sheet and bake in a preheated moderately hot oven (190°C/375°F, Gas Mark 5) for 15 minutes or until golden brown.

Meanwhile melt the remaining butter in a pan and sauté the onion until soft. Add the wine, bring to the boil and continue boiling until the liquid is reduced by half. Add the cream and heat to reduce by half again.

Detach the corals from the scallops and cut the white meat in half. Place all the scallop pieces in the reduced liquid and poach for 3 minutes.

Allow to cool slightly, then stir in the egg yolks and salt and pepper to taste. Spoon the mixture into the croustades.

Whisk the egg whites until stiff and fold in the cheese. Place in a piping (pastry) bag fitted with a plain 1 cm/½ inch nozzle. Pipe the meringue onto the croustades. Cook in a preheated moderately hot oven (200°C/400°F, Gas Mark 6) for 10 to 15 minutes or until the meringue is golden and crisp.

Serve hot, garnished with cayenne and watercress.
Cooking time: 50 minutes to 1 hour
Serves 4

Poisson en Brochette

METRIC/IMPERIAL	AMERICAN
100 g/4 oz button onions, peeled	¼ lb pearl onions, peeled
salt and pepper	salt and pepper
100 g/4 oz courgettes, cut into chunks	¼ lb zucchini, cut into chunks
225 g/8 oz streaky bacon, derinded	½ lb fatty bacon slices, rinds removed
225 g/8 oz opened mussels	½ lb shucked mussels
450 g/1 lb monkfish, skinned and cubed	1 lb monkfish, skinned and cubed
100 g/4 oz button mushrooms	1 cup button mushrooms
bay leaves	bay leaves
50 g/2 oz butter, melted	¼ cup melted butter
To serve:	**To serve:**
boiled rice	boiled rice
tomato sauce	tomato sauce

Blanch the onions in boiling salted water for 2 minutes. Add the courgettes (zucchini) and blanch for 2 minutes; drain.

Stretch the bacon rashers with the back of a knife, cut in half and wrap a piece around each mussel.

Arrange all the ingredients on 4 skewers and sprinkle with salt and pepper. Brush with the melted butter and cook under a preheated moderate grill (broiler) for 6 to 8 minutes. Turn over, brush with butter again and grill (broil) for a further 6 to 8 minutes or until cooked.

Arrange the skewers on a bed of rice and serve with a tomato sauce.
Cooking time: 25 minutes
Serves 4

Sprats (Smelts) Boursin

METRIC/IMPERIAL	AMERICAN
450 g/1 lb sprats	1 lb smelts
salt and pepper	salt and pepper
150 g/5 oz Boursin cream cheese	⅔ cup Boursin cream cheese
a little plain flour	a little all-purpose flour
2 eggs, beaten	2 eggs, beaten
fresh breadcrumbs, to coat	soft bread crumbs, for coating
oil for deep fat frying	oil for deep fat frying
parsley to garnish	parsley for garnish

Clean and remove the heads from the sprats (smelts). To remove the backbone, slit along the belly, open the fish and place, skin uppermost, on a board. Press firmly along the back of the fish, turn over and remove the bone. Wash and dry on kitchen paper towels.

Sprinkle the fish with salt and pepper. Soften the cheese and spread inside each fish. Fold over to reform the shape of a sprat (smelt). Dust with flour, dip in beaten egg and coat in breadcrumbs.

Heat the oil to 180°C/350°F and fry the fish for 4 minutes. Drain on kitchen paper towels and arrange on a hot serving dish. Serve immediately garnished with parsley.
Cooking time: 4 minutes
Serves 4 to 6

Fish Lyonnaise

METRIC/IMPERIAL	AMERICAN
25 g/1 oz butter	2 tablespoons butter
2 large onions, finely sliced	2 large onions, finely sliced
salt and pepper	salt and pepper
½ teaspoon sugar	½ teaspoon sugar
750 g/1½ lb whole plaice	1½ lb whole flounder
150 ml/¼ pint dry white wine	⅔ cup dry white wine
7 tablespoons water	7 tablespoons water
1 teaspoon mushroom essence	1 teaspoon mushroom extract
1 teaspoon lemon juice	1 teaspoon lemon juice
chopped parsley to garnish	chopped parsley for garnish
Beurre manié:	**Beurre manié:**
15 g/½ oz butter	1 tablespoon butter
15 g/½ oz plain flour	2 tablespoons all-purpose flour

Melt the butter in a large pan, add the onions, salt and pepper to taste and sugar. Sauté until soft but not brown.

Wash, trim and dry the fish, score across the bone and lay fish on top of the onions with the dark skin uppermost. Add the wine, water, mushroom essence, and lemon juice. Cover and simmer gently for 20 minutes, basting every 5 to 10 minutes.

Carefully remove the fish and lift off the skin. Arrange on a hot serving dish and surround with the onions. Keep warm.

To make the beurre manié: blend together the butter and flour. Add a small piece to the liquor in the pan and whisk thoroughly.

Continue whisking in small pieces of the beurre manié. Heat the sauce, stirring all the time until it thickens, then spoon over the fish.

Serve garnished with parsley.
Cooking time: 35 minutes
Serves 4

Whiting with Provençal Sauce

METRIC/IMPERIAL	AMERICAN
750 g/1½ lb whiting fillets, skinned	1½ lb whiting fillets, skinned
50 g/2 oz plain flour, seasoned with salt and pepper	½ cup all-purpose flour, seasoned with salt and pepper
3 tablespoons oil	3 tablespoons oil
Sauce:	**Sauce:**
25 g/1 oz butter	2 tablespoons butter
1 small onion, finely chopped	1 small onion, finely chopped
1 clove garlic, crushed	1 clove garlic, crushed
100 g/4 oz mushrooms, sliced	1 cup sliced mushrooms
25 g/1 oz plain flour	¼ cup all-purpose flour
1 × 227 g/8 oz can tomatoes	1 × 8 oz can tomatoes
1 tablespoon tomato purée	1 tablespoon tomato paste
300 ml/½ pint fish stock	1¼ cups fish stock
1 tablespoon dry sherry	1 tablespoon dry sherry
1 teaspoon dried oregano	1 teaspoon dried oregano
salt and pepper	salt and pepper
parsley to garnish	parsley for garnish

To make the sauce: melt the butter in a pan and sauté the onion, garlic and mushrooms for 10 minutes. Stir in the flour and cook for 1 minute. Add the tomatoes with their juice, tomato purée (paste), stock and sherry. Bring to the boil, stirring, then add the oregano and salt and pepper to taste. Cover and simmer for 10 to 15 minutes.

Meanwhile coat the fish in the seasoned flour. Heat the oil in a frying pan and fry the fish for 10 minutes or until golden brown all over. Drain on kitchen paper towels.

Arrange the fish on a warm serving platter and pour over some of the sauce and serve the remainder separately. Garnish with parsley.
Cooking time: 30 to 40 minutes
Serves 4

Fish à la Crème

METRIC/IMPERIAL	AMERICAN
8 × 75 g/3 oz John Dory or flat fish fillets	8 × 3 oz flounder fillets
50 g/2 oz plain flour	½ cup all-purpose flour
salt and pepper	salt and pepper
50 g/2 oz butter	¼ cup butter
1 bunch spring onions, chopped	1 bunch scallions, chopped
150 ml/¼ pint milk	⅔ cup milk
150 ml/¼ pint single cream	⅔ cup light cream
100 g/4 oz peeled prawns	⅔ cup shelled shrimp

Wash and dry the fish fillets. Season the flour with salt and pepper then sprinkle over the fillets.

Melt the butter in a frying pan and cook the fish for 2 to 3 minutes.

Add the spring onions (scallions), milk and cream and simmer gently for 8 minutes. Just before serving, add the prawns (shrimp) and heat through until piping hot.

Check the seasoning and spoon into a warm serving dish.
Cooking time: 15 to 20 minutes
Serves 4

Red Mullet à la Moutarde

METRIC/IMPERIAL	AMERICAN
4 red mullet	4 red mullet
1 small onion, finely chopped	1 small onion, finely chopped
1 clove garlic, crushed	1 clove garlic, crushed
2 tablespoons lemon juice	2 tablespoons lemon juice
3 tablespoons chopped parsley	3 tablespoons chopped parsley
salt and pepper	salt and pepper
Mustard butter:	**Mustard butter:**
50 g/2 oz butter	¼ cup butter
4 teaspoons French mustard	4 teaspoons Dijon-style mustard
1 teaspoon lemon juice	1 teaspoon lemon juice
½ teaspoon dried mixed herbs	½ teaspoon dried mixed herbs
Garnish:	**Garnish:**
parsley	parsley

Split the fish along the belly and lay flat, skin side uppermost. Press along the backbones, turn the fish over and remove the backbone with as many small bones as possible.

Arrange the fish in a greased shallow ovenproof dish, flesh side uppermost. Sprinkle with the onion, garlic, lemon juice, parsley and salt and pepper to taste. Cook in a preheated moderate oven (180°C/350°F, Gas Mark 4) for 20 to 25 minutes or until the fish are just tender.

To make the mustard butter: blend together all the ingredients and form into 4 neat portions.

Arrange the cooked fish on a warm serving dish and garnish with parsley. Place a pat of mustard butter on each fish.
Cooking time: 20 to 25 minutes
Serves 4

Moules Marinière

METRIC/IMPERIAL	AMERICAN
25 g/1 oz butter	2 tablespoons butter
1 onion, finely chopped	1 onion, finely chopped
1 clove garlic, crushed	1 clove garlic, crushed
300 ml/½ pint dry white wine	1¼ cups dry white wine
2 tablespoons lemon juice	2 tablespoons lemon juice
3 fresh bay leaves	3 fresh bay leaves
salt and pepper	salt and pepper
3.5 litres/6 pints live mussels, scrubbed	4 quarts live mussels, scrubbed
6 tablespoons chopped parsley	6 tablespoons chopped parsley

Melt the butter in a large pan and sauté the onion and garlic for 5 minutes. Add the wine, lemon juice, bay leaves and salt and pepper to taste. Bring to the boil and add the mussels all at once. Cover and cook over a high heat, shaking the pan occasionally, for 5 to 10 minutes or until all the mussels have opened. Remove the bay leaves and any mussels that have not opened.

Drain the mussels, reserving the liquor, and transfer to a warm serving dish. Boil the liquor for 5 minutes, then add salt and pepper and the parsley. Pour over the mussels and serve with French bread.
Cooking time: 15 to 20 minutes
Serves 4 to 6

Moules Marinière
(Photograph: Sea Fish Kitchen)

Devilled Crab

METRIC/IMPERIAL	AMERICAN
50 g/2 oz fresh breadcrumbs	1 cup soft bread crumbs
120 ml/4 fl oz milk	½ cup milk
150 g/5 oz crabmeat, flaked	⅔ cup flaked crab meat
2 egg yolks	2 egg yolks
75 g/3 oz butter, melted	6 tablespoons melted butter
2 teaspoons made mustard	2 teaspoons prepared mustard
¼ teaspoon ground mace	¼ teaspoon ground mace
2 tablespoons chopped parsley	2 tablespoons chopped parsley
salt and pepper	salt and pepper
Topping:	**Topping:**
20 g/¾ oz fresh breadcrumbs	⅓ cup soft bread crumbs
1 tablespoon chopped parsley	1 tablespoon chopped parsley
15 g/½ oz butter	1 tablespoon butter
Garnish:	**Garnish:**
lemon slices	lemon slices
watercress	watercress

Soak the breadcrumbs in the milk for 15 minutes then mix with the crabmeat. Add the egg yolks, butter, mustard, mace, parsley and salt and pepper to taste. Mix well and spoon the mixture into 4 cleaned and oiled scallop or crab shells.

For the topping: mix together the breadcrumbs and parsley. Sprinkle them over the crab mixture and dot with the butter. Cook in a preheated hot oven (230°C/450°F, Gas Mark 8) for 10 to 15 minutes or until well browned. Serve hot, garnished with lemon slices and watercress.

Cooking time: 10 to 15 minutes
Serves 4

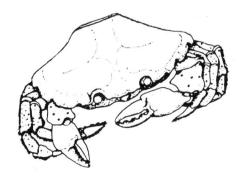

Seafood Crêpes

METRIC/IMPERIAL	AMERICAN
Pancakes:	**Crêpes:**
100 g/4 oz plain flour	1 cup all-purpose flour
½ teaspoon salt	½ teaspoon salt
1 egg, beaten	1 egg, beaten
300 ml/½ pint milk	1¼ cups milk
oil	oil
Filling:	**Filling:**
225 g/8 oz white fish	½ lb white fish
100 g/4 oz peeled prawns	⅔ cup shelled shrimp
300 ml/½ pint milk	1¼ cups milk
25 g/1 oz butter	2 tablespoons butter
25 g/1 oz plain flour	¼ cup all-purpose flour
salt and pepper	salt and pepper
4 ripe tomatoes, skinned	4 ripe tomatoes, peeled
1 tablespoon lemon juice	1 tablespoon lemon juice
parsley to garnish	parsley for garnish

To make the pancakes: sift the flour and salt into a bowl. Make a well in the centre and add the egg and half the milk. Beat with a wooden spoon until smooth, then gradually blend in the remaining milk. Pour the batter into a jug.

Oil an 18 cm/7 inch non-stick frying pan and place over a moderate heat. Add enough batter to cover the base of the pan. Heat until cooked and golden on the underside. Toss or turn and cook the other side. Make 7 more pancakes and keep them hot by stacking, interleaved with greaseproof (waxed) paper, in a pile on a plate, then place the plate over a pan of hot water.

To make the filling: place the white fish, prawns (shrimp) and half the milk in a pan. Cover and simmer for 5 minutes or until the fish flakes. Remove the fish and prawns (shrimp) with a slotted spoon and reserve the liquid. Flake the fish and remove any skin and bones.

In a clean pan, melt the butter and stir in the flour. Cook for 1 minute then remove from the heat. Gradually stir in the milk liquor and the remaining milk. Cook, stirring, until the sauce thickens, then add salt and pepper to taste.

Chop the tomatoes and add to the sauce with the fish, prawns (shrimp) and lemon juice. Adjust the seasoning and use the mixture to fill the pancakes. Fold over and arrange in a hot serving dish. Garnish with parsley.

Cooking time: 35 to 40 minutes
Serves 4

Salmon Mousse

METRIC/IMPERIAL
25 g/1 oz butter
25 g/1 oz plain flour
300 ml/½ pint milk
salt and pepper
2 eggs, separated
1 tablespoon gelatine
1 tablespoon lemon
   juice
3 tablespoons water
225 g/8 oz cooked
   salmon, flaked
1 tablespoon tomato
   purée
150 ml/¼ pint double
   cream
cucumber slices to
   garnish

AMERICAN
2 tablespoons butter
¼ cup all-purpose
   flour
1¼ cups milk
salt and pepper
2 eggs, separated
1 tablespoon
   unflavored gelatin
1 tablespoon lemon
   juice
3 tablespoons water
½ lb cooked flaked
   salmon
1 tablespoon tomato
   paste
⅔ cup heavy cream
cucumber slices for
   garnish

Melt the butter in a pan, stir in the flour and cook for 1 minute. Remove from the heat and gradually blend in the milk. Return to the heat and cook, stirring, until the sauce thickens. Add salt and pepper to taste. Stir in the egg yolks and heat through gently, then allow the sauce to cool.

Sprinkle the gelatine over the lemon juice and water in a heatproof bowl. Place the bowl over a pan of gently simmering water and stir until the gelatine dissolves. Cool slightly and stir into the sauce mixture with the salmon and tomato purée (paste).

Whip the cream until thick and fold into the mixture. Whisk the egg whites until stiff and fold in gently. Adjust the seasoning and pour the mixture into a wetted 900 ml/1½ pint (5 cup) mould or dish. Chill in the refrigerator until set.

To serve the mousse, dip the mould into boiling water then invert onto a serving platter. Garnish with cucumber and serve with a green salad.
Cooking time: 20 minutes
Serves 4 to 6

Stuffed Sea Bream (Porgy)

METRIC/IMPERIAL
1 × 1.75 kg/4 lb sea
   bream
150 g/5 oz butter
2 onions, chopped
225 g/8 oz long grain
   rice
600 ml/1 pint water
1 teaspoon salt
175 g/6 oz
   mushrooms, sliced
2 teaspoons chopped
   tarragon
1 teaspoon chopped
   mint
1 teaspoon chopped
   sage
3 teaspoons chopped
   parsley
pepper
juice of 1 lemon
Garnish:
lemon slices
parsley sprigs

AMERICAN
1 × 4 lb porgy or
   ocean perch
⅔ cup butter
2 onions, chopped
½ lb long grain rice
2½ cups water
1 teaspoon salt
1½ cups sliced
   mushrooms
2 teaspoons chopped
   tarragon
1 teaspoon chopped
   mint
1 teaspoon chopped
   sage
3 teaspoons chopped
   parsley
pepper
juice of 1 lemon
Garnish:
lemon slices
parsley sprigs

Scale and clean the fish but keep whole. Melt 50 g/2 oz (¼ cup) butter in a pan and sauté the onions for 3 minutes. Add the rice and cook for 1 minute, then stir in the water and salt. Bring to the boil and add the mushrooms. Cover and simmer for 15 minutes, or until the rice is tender and the liquid absorbed. Stir in the herbs and salt and pepper to taste.

Sprinkle the inside of the fish with salt and pepper and the outside with lemon juice, salt and pepper. Place the fish in a large greased roasting pan, then fill the fish with the rice mixture. Secure with wooden cocktail sticks (toothpicks). Dot with the remaining butter and cook in a preheated moderately hot oven (190°C/375°F, Gas Mark 5) for 30 minutes, basting frequently.

Place the fish on a warm serving platter. Remove the cocktail sticks (toothpicks) and garnish with lemon slices and parsley.
Cooking time: 55 minutes
Serves 4

Meat & Poultry Dishes

Steak Flambé with Liver and Brandy Sauce

METRIC/IMPERIAL	AMERICAN
25 g/1 oz butter	2 tablespoons butter
4 fillet steaks	4 fillet steaks
150 ml/¼ pint beef stock	⅔ cup beef stock
100 g/4 oz liver pâté	½ cup liver pâté
salt and pepper	salt and pepper
4 tablespoons brandy	4 tablespoons brandy
watercress to garnish	watercress for garnish

Melt the butter in a frying pan and brown the meat for 2 minutes on each side, then remove. Add the stock and pâté to the pan and stir until a thick purée is formed. Add salt and pepper to taste.

Return the meat to the pan and heat gently for 5 minutes. Warm the brandy in a pan or a ladle, ignite and pour over the steaks. Shake the pan so that the flames spread and burn for as long as possible. This will ensure that the steaks are cooked.

Arrange the steaks on a warm serving dish and spoon the sauce over. Serve hot, garnished with watercress.

Cooking time: 15 to 20 minutes
Serves 4

Boeuf en Croûte

METRIC/IMPERIAL	AMERICAN
1.5 kg (3 lb) fillet beef	3 lb beef tenderloin
1 tablespoon oil	1 tablespoon oil
salt and pepper	salt and pepper
40 g/1½ oz butter	3 tablespoons butter
450 g/1 lb mushrooms, finely chopped	4 cups finely chopped mushrooms
1 small onion, finely chopped	1 small onion, finely chopped
4 tablespoons horseradish mustard	4 tablespoons horseradish mustard
450 g/1 lb frozen puff pastry, thawed	1 lb frozen puff pastry, thawed
beaten egg to glaze	beaten egg for glaze

Rub the beef all over with the oil, salt and pepper. Put on a rack and roast in a preheated hot oven (230°C/450°F, Gas Mark 8) for 40 minutes. Remove and leave until cold.

Melt the butter in a frying pan and gently cook the mushrooms and onion until tender. Drain well. Mix the mustard with the mushrooms and onion to make a paste.

Roll out the pastry to a rectangle 5 mm/ ¼ inch thick and large enough to enclose the meat. Dampen the edges. Spread the mustard mixture over the fillet and place on the pastry. Wrap the pastry round the beef to make a neat parcel and seal all the edges well together. Place the beef, seam side down, on a baking sheet. Roll out the trimmings to make pastry leaves and arrange on the beef roll. Brush with beaten egg, pierce pastry in three places and cook in a preheated hot oven (230°C/450°F, Gas Mark 8) for 40 minutes or until golden brown.

Cooking time: 1 hour 40 minutes
Serves 6

Boeuf en Croûte
(Photograph: Colman's Mustard)

Beef Chasseur

METRIC/IMPERIAL	AMERICAN
1 tablespoon oil	1 tablespoon oil
25 g/1 oz butter	2 tablespoons butter
750 g/1½ lb braising steak, cubed	1½ lb braising steak, cubed
1 onion, finely chopped	1 onion, finely chopped
1 clove garlic, crushed	1 clove garlic, crushed
25 g/1 oz plain flour	¼ cup all-purpose flour
300 ml/½ pint beef stock	1¼ cups beef stock
1 tablespoon soft brown sugar	1 tablespoon light brown sugar
1 × 227 g/8 oz can tomatoes	1 × 8 oz can tomatoes
1 teaspoon tomato purée	1 teaspoon tomato paste
300 ml/½ pint red wine	1¼ cups red wine
salt and pepper	salt and pepper
100 g/4 oz button mushrooms	1 cup button mushrooms
parsley to garnish	parsley for garnish

Heat the oil and butter in a large saucepan, then fry the meat for 5 minutes to brown the meat on all sides. Remove with a slotted spoon and leave on one side.

Add the onion and garlic to the pan and sauté for 5 minutes. Stir in the flour and cook for 1 minute. Remove from the heat and gradually blend in the stock. Return to the heat, stirring all the time, until the sauce thickens. Stir in the sugar, tomatoes with their juice, tomato purée (paste), wine and salt and pepper to taste. Replace the meat, bring to the boil, cover and simmer for 1½ hours. Add the mushrooms and continue to cook for 30 minutes. Serve hot, garnished with parsley.
Cooking time: 2¼ hours
Serves 4

Beef Olives with Spring Onions (Scallions) and Mushrooms

METRIC/IMPERIAL	AMERICAN
50 g/2 oz butter	¼ cup butter
4 fillet steaks, rolled	4 fillet steaks, rolled
2 teaspoons tomato purée	2 teaspoons tomato paste
2 teaspoons meat extract	2 teaspoons meat extract
150 ml/¼ pint water	⅔ cup water
salt and pepper	salt and pepper
1 bunch spring onions	1 bunch scallions
100 g/4 oz button mushrooms	1 cup button mushrooms
4 tablespoons single cream	4 tablespoons light cream
chopped parsley to garnish	chopped parsley for garnish

Melt half the butter in a pan and cook the steaks for 10 minutes, turning frequently. Add the tomato purée (paste) and meat extract, then continue to cook for 1 minute. Add the water, salt and pepper.

Trim the spring onions (scallions) and wash with the mushrooms; dry well. Melt the remaining butter in a separate pan and sauté the onions and mushrooms for 3 minutes, then add to the meat.

Bring to the boil, cover and simmer for 25 minutes. Stir in the cream and adjust the seasoning. Arrange the beef olives and vegetables on a warm serving dish and spoon the sauce over. Garnish with parsley and serve with savoury rice.
Cooking time: 40 to 45 minutes
Serves 4

Veal Suprême

METRIC/IMPERIAL	AMERICAN
1 large onion, sliced	1 large onion, sliced
3 sticks celery, chopped	3 stalks celery, chopped
3 carrots, sliced	3 carrots, sliced
750 g/1½ lb stewing veal, cubed	1½ lb boneless veal for stew, cubed
salt and pepper	salt and pepper
1 bouquet garni	1 bouquet garni
300 ml/½ pint chicken stock	1¼ cups chicken stock or broth
3 teaspoons cornflour	3 teaspoons cornstarch
2 tablespoons water	2 tablespoons water
4 tablespoons single cream	4 tablespoons light cream
Garnish:	**Garnish:**
4 bacon rolls	4 bacon rolls
chopped parsley	chopped parsley

Place the onion, celery and carrot in a casserole dish. Arrange the veal on top and sprinkle liberally with salt and pepper. Add the bouquet garni and stock. Cover and cook in a preheated moderate oven (160°C/325°F, Gas Mark 3) for 1½ hours.

Blend the cornflour (cornstarch) with the water and stir into the casserole. Return to the oven for 20 minutes.

Just before serving, remove the bouquet garni, adjust the seasoning and stir in the cream. Garnish with bacon rolls and parsley.
Cooking time: 1 hour 50 minutes
Serves 4

Lamb Citron

METRIC/IMPERIAL	AMERICAN
450 g/1 lb lamb fillet	1 lb lamb fillet
2 tablespoons plain flour	2 tablespoons all-purpose flour
salt and pepper	salt and pepper
2 tablespoons oil	2 tablespoons oil
4 tablespoons beef stock	4 tablespoons beef stock
½ lemon, thinly sliced	½ lemon, thinly sliced
2 teaspoons lemon juice	2 teaspoons lemon juice
15 g/½ oz butter	1 tablespoon butter
Garnish:	**Garnish:**
lemon slices	lemon slices
watercress	watercress

Slice the lamb thinly and pound the slices to make them flatter. Mix the flour, salt and pepper, then sprinkle over the meat. Heat the oil in a pan, add the meat and brown on both sides.

Add the stock and place the lemon slices over the meat. Bring to the boil, cover and simmer for 10 to 15 minutes. Remove the lamb with a slotted spoon. Place on a warm serving platter and keep warm. Add the lemon juice and butter to the pan with salt and pepper to taste. Heat through and spoon over the meat. Garnish with lemon slices and watercress.
Cooking time: 20 to 25 minutes
Serves 4

Lamb and White Wine Casserole

METRIC/IMPERIAL	AMERICAN
3 tablespoons plain flour	3 tablespoons all-purpose flour
salt and pepper	salt and pepper
750 g/1½ lb boned shoulder of lamb, cubed	1½ lb boneless lamb for stew, cubed
2 tablespoons oil	2 tablespoons oil
2 cloves garlic, crushed	2 cloves garlic, crushed
300 ml/½ pint dry white wine	1¼ cups dry white wine
1 bay leaf	1 bay leaf
2 egg yolks, beaten	2 egg yolks, beaten
1 tablespoon lemon juice	1 tablespoon lemon juice
chopped parsley to garnish	chopped parsley for garnish

Season the flour with salt and pepper. Place the meat in a bowl, add the flour and toss until the meat is well coated.

Heat the oil in a pan and fry the meat with the garlic until browned all over. Remove the meat with a slotted spoon and place in a casserole dish. Add the wine, bay leaf and salt and pepper to taste. Cover and cook in a preheated cool oven (150°C/300°F, Gas Mark 2) for 2 hours.

Just before serving, stir in the egg yolks and lemon juice. Sprinkle with parsley and serve with rice or new potatoes.
Cooking time: 2 hours 10 minutes
Serves 4

Garlic Marinated Lamb

METRIC/IMPERIAL	AMERICAN
4 lamb chump chops	4 lamb sirloin steaks
Marinade:	**Marinade:**
2 teaspoons oil	2 teaspoons oil
1 tablespoon soy sauce	1 tablespoon soy sauce
2 cloves garlic, crushed	2 cloves garlic, crushed
salt and pepper	salt and pepper
Sauce:	**Sauce:**
1 tablespoon oil	1 tablespoon oil
1 onion, sliced	1 onion, sliced
1 × 227 g/8 oz can, tomatoes	1 × 8 oz can tomatoes
½ green pepper, cored, seeded and diced	½ green pepper, seeded and diced
½ teaspoon mixed herbs	½ teaspoon mixed herbs
1 teaspoon lemon juice	1 teaspoon lemon juice
salt and pepper	salt and pepper
50 g/2 oz mushrooms, chopped	½ cup chopped mushrooms
parsley to garnish	parsley for garnish

Mix together the marinade ingredients and place the chops in it for 2 to 3 hours; drain.

Cook the chops under a preheated moderate grill (broiler) for 10 to 15 minutes on each side.

Meanwhile make the sauce: heat the oil in a pan and sauté the onion for 5 minutes. Add the tomatoes with their juice, green pepper, herbs, lemon juice and salt and pepper to taste. Bring to the boil, cover and simmer for 20 minutes. Add the mushrooms and continue to cook for 5 minutes.

Arrange the lamb chops on a warm serving dish and spoon the sauce over. Garnish with parsley.
Cooking time: 30 minutes
Serves 4

Noisettes of Lamb

METRIC/IMPERIAL	AMERICAN
50 g/2 oz butter	¼ cup butter
1 tablespoon oil	1 tablespoon oil
8 noisettes of lamb, prepared from the loin	8 boneless double loin lamb chops
1 large onion, finely chopped	1 large onion, finely chopped
1 clove garlic, crushed	1 clove garlic, crushed
450 g/1 lb tomatoes, skinned and chopped	1 lb tomatoes, peeled and chopped
1 tablespoon tomato purée	1 tablespoon tomato paste
150 ml/¼ pint dry white wine	⅔ cup dry white wine
salt and freshly ground black pepper	salt and freshly ground black pepper
1 tablespoon chopped parsley to garnish	1 tablespoon chopped parsley for garnish

Heat half the butter and half the oil in a pan and sauté the lamb for about 15 minutes.

Meanwhile heat the remaining butter and oil in another pan and fry the onion and garlic gently until soft. Add the tomatoes, tomato purée (paste) and wine to the onion and bring to the boil, stirring. Cook, uncovered, over a brisk heat for 10 to 15 minutes, stirring occasionally. Season to taste with salt and pepper.

Place the lamb on a serving dish, pour over the sauce and sprinkle with parsley.
Cooking time: 40 minutes
Serves 4

Noisettes of Lamb
(Photograph: New Zealand Lamb Information Bureau)

Cassoulet

METRIC/IMPERIAL
1 tablespoon oil
1 large onion, sliced
100 g/4 oz bacon, chopped
1 kg/2 lb belly pork, cubed
100 g/4 oz dried butter beans, soaked overnight
225 g/8 oz garlic sausage, cubed
750 ml/1¼ pints stock
1 × 227 g/8 oz can tomatoes
bouquet garni
salt and pepper
75 g/3 oz fresh breadcrumbs

AMERICAN
1 tablespoon oil
1 large onion, sliced
¼ lb fatty bacon slices, chopped
2 lb fresh pork sides, cubed
⅔ cup dried butter beans, soaked overnight
½ lb garlic sausage, cubed
3 cups stock
1 × 8 oz can tomatoes
bouquet garni
salt and pepper
1½ cups fresh bread crumbs

Heat the oil in a pan and fry the onion and bacon for 3 minutes. Add the pork and continue to cook for 5 minutes, turning the meat to brown evenly.

Drain the butter beans and add to the pan with the garlic sausage, stock, tomatoes with their juice, bouquet garni and salt and pepper to taste. Bring to the boil, stirring, and boil for 10 minutes. Transfer to a 2.25 litre/4 pint (2½ quart) casserole dish.

Cover and cook in a preheated moderate oven (160°C/325°F, Gas Mark 3) for 1½ hours. Remove the bouquet garni and adjust the seasoning. Sprinkle with the breadcrumbs and return to the oven, uncovered, for another hour. Serve hot.
Cooking time: 2 hours 50 minutes
Serves 4 to 6

Pork Chops Dijonnaise

METRIC/IMPERIAL
1 kg/2 lb potatoes, peeled
1 large onion, peeled
finely grated rind of ½ orange
1 teaspoon dried sage
300 ml/½ pint stock
salt and pepper
4 pork chops
4 teaspoons Dijon mustard
4 tablespoons single cream
chopped parsley to garnish

AMERICAN
2 lb potatoes, peeled
1 large onion, peeled
finely grated rind of ½ orange
1 teaspoon dried sage
1¼ cups stock
salt and pepper
4 center cut pork chops
4 teaspoons Dijon mustard
4 tablespoons light cream
chopped parsley for garnish

Chop the potatoes and onion finely. Place in a greased, shallow ovenproof dish. Mix in the orange rind, sage, stock and salt and pepper to taste.

Wash and trim the chops and arrange on top of the vegetables. Cover with foil and cook in a preheated moderately hot oven (190°C/375°F, Gas Mark 5) for 40 minutes. Remove the foil and increase the temperature to 200°C/400°F, Gas Mark 6. Cook for a further 30 minutes or until the meat and vegetables are cooked through.

Remove the chops and keep hot. Mix together the mustard and cream and stir into the vegetables. Arrange vegetables around the edge of a warm serving platter and place the chops in the centre. Garnish with parsley.
Cooking time: 1¼ hours
Serves 4

Normandy Pork

METRIC/IMPERIAL	AMERICAN
25 g/1 oz butter	2 tablespoons butter
350 g/12 oz lean pork, cubed	¾ lb pork tenderloin, cubed
1 onion, chopped	1 onion, chopped
1 dessert apple, peeled, cored and sliced	1 dessert apple, peeled, cored and sliced
300 ml/½ pint cider	1¼ cups hard cider
600 ml/1 pint stock	2½ cups stock
225 g/8 oz long grain rice	1 cup + 2 tablespoons long grain rice
salt and pepper	salt and pepper
4 tablespoons double cream	4 tablespoons heavy cream
chopped parsley to garnish	chopped parsley for garnish

Melt the butter in a large pan and fry the meat over a fairly high heat for 15 minutes or until browned all over and nearly cooked through. Add the onion and sauté for 5 minutes, then add the apple.

Stir in the cider, stock, rice and salt and pepper to taste. Bring to the boil, then transfer to a casserole dish. Cover and cook in a preheated moderate oven (180°C/350°F, Gas Mark 4) for 30 minutes or until the rice is tender. Remove from the oven, adjust the seasoning and stir in the cream just before serving. Sprinkle with parsley.
Cooking time: 50 minutes to 1 hour
Serves 4

Pork Boulangère

METRIC/IMPERIAL	AMERICAN
1.75 kg/4 lb hand of pork	4 lb hand of pork
oil	oil
salt and pepper	salt and pepper
1 kg/2 lb potatoes, peeled	2 lb potatoes, peeled
3 onions, peeled	3 onions, peeled
450 g/1 lb courgettes	1 lb zucchini
300 ml/½ pint chicken stock	1¼ cups chicken stock or broth
1 clove garlic, crushed	1 clove garlic, crushed
1 sprig fresh thyme	1 sprig fresh thyme

Score the pork rind and rub oil and salt into the skin. Cook in a preheated hot oven (220°C/425°F, Gas Mark 7) for 1 hour. Remove from the oven and place the meat on a dish.

Slice the potatoes, onions and courgettes (zucchini) and place in the roasting pan with the potatoes on top. Place the meat on top. Mix the chicken stock with the garlic and thyme, then pour over the vegetables. Add salt and pepper to taste, then return to a moderately hot oven (190°C/375°F, Gas Mark 5) for 1¼ hours.
Cooking time: 2¼ hours
Serves 4

French Turkey with Roquefort and Pâté Stuffing

METRIC/IMPERIAL	AMERICAN
1 × 3 kg/7 lb turkey, cleaned	1 × 7 lb turkey, cleaned
2 tablespoons brandy, warmed	2 tablespoons brandy, warmed
50 g/2 oz butter, melted	¼ cup melted butter
salt and pepper	salt and pepper
300 ml/½ pint dry white wine	1¼ cups dry white wine
150 ml/¼ pint double cream	⅔ cup heavy cream
Stuffing:	**Stuffing:**
100 g/4 oz Roquefort cheese, crumbled	1 cup crumbled Roquefort cheese
100 g/4 oz liver pâté	¼ lb liver pâté
100 g/4 oz fresh breadcrumbs	2 cups soft bread crumbs
1 tablespoon chopped parsley	1 tablespoon chopped parsley
salt and pepper	salt and pepper

To make the stuffing: mix together the cheese, pâté, breadcrumbs, parsley and salt and pepper to taste. Mix well and stuff into neck end of turkey. Sew up with a trussing needle.

Place the turkey in a roasting pan, pour the brandy over and ignite. Brush with the melted butter and season with salt and pepper. Add the wine and cover with foil. Cook in a preheated moderate oven (160°C/325°F, Gas Mark 3) for 3½ hours. Remove the foil and continue to cook for 30 minutes.

Place the turkey on a warm serving platter and keep hot. Stir the cream into the juices in the pan. Heat gently, then strain into a jug and serve with the turkey.
Cooking time: 4 hours
Serves 6 to 8

Turkey Olives

METRIC/IMPERIAL	AMERICAN
4 turkey escalopes	4 turkey escalopes
oil for frying	oil for frying
Stuffing:	**Stuffing:**
50 g/2 oz fresh breadcrumbs	1 cup soft bread crumbs
grated rind of ½ orange	grated rind of ½ orange
8 stuffed olives, sliced	8 stuffed olives, sliced
40 g/1½ oz cooked ham, chopped	3 tablespoons chopped cooked ham
salt and pepper	salt and pepper
25 g/1 oz margarine	2 tablespoons margarine
1 small onion, finely chopped	1 small onion, finely chopped
Sauce:	**Sauce:**
15 g/½ oz butter	1 tablespoon butter
1 onion, chopped	1 onion, chopped
1 clove garlic, crushed	1 clove garlic, crushed
2 teaspoons plain flour	2 teaspoons all-purpose flour
3 tablespoons orange juice	3 tablespoons orange juice
150 ml/¼ pint stock	⅔ cup stock
1 × 283 g/10 oz can creamed sweetcorn	1 × 10 oz can creamed kernel corn
salt and pepper	salt and pepper
Garnish:	**Garnish:**
stuffed olive slices	stuffed olive slices
orange slices	orange slices
parsley sprigs	parsley sprigs

Place the turkey escalopes between 2 pieces of plastic wrap and beat until thin.

To make the stuffing: mix together the breadcrumbs, orange rind, olives, ham and salt and pepper to taste. Melt the margarine in a pan and sauté the onion for 5 minutes. Stir into the stuffing to bind together.

Divide the stuffing between the escalopes and roll up, securing with cocktail sticks (toothpicks). Heat the oil in a frying pan and fry the turkey olives gently for 10 to 15 minutes, turning, until almost cooked through. Remove with a slotted spoon and place in a greased, shallow ovenproof dish. Cook in a preheated moderate oven (180°C/350°F, Gas Mark 4) for 15 minutes.

To make the sauce: heat the butter with the oil in the frying pan, then sauté the onion and garlic for 5 minutes. Stir in the flour and cook for 1 minute. Gradually blend in the orange juice and stock. Heat the sauce, stirring, until it thickens. Stir in the corn and salt and pepper to taste. Heat through gently and pour over the turkey olives. Return to the oven for 15 minutes. Serve hot, garnished with olives, orange slices and parsley.

Cooking time: about 1 hour
Serves 4

Gascony Turkey

METRIC/IMPERIAL	AMERICAN
50 g/2 oz butter	¼ cup butter
1 large onion, chopped	1 large onion, chopped
4 turkey fillets	4 turkey fillets
100 g/4 oz mushrooms, sliced	1 cup sliced mushrooms
40 g/1½ oz plain flour	6 tablespoons all-purpose flour
450 ml/¾ pint chicken stock	2 cups chicken stock or broth
finely grated rind and juice of ½ lemon	finely grated rind and juice of ½ lemon
50 g/2 oz gherkins, chopped	⅓ cup chopped gherkins
2 tablespoons chopped parsley	2 tablespoons chopped parsley
salt and pepper	salt and pepper
4 tablespoons double cream	4 tablespoons heavy cream

Melt the butter in a frying pan and sauté the onion for 5 minutes. Add the turkey and fry on both sides until browned. Remove with a slotted spoon.

Add the mushrooms and sauté for 3 minutes. Stir in the flour and cook for 1 minute. Gradually blend in the stock, lemon rind and juice. Bring to the boil, then stir in the gherkins, parsley and salt and pepper to taste. Replace the turkey fillets, cover and simmer for 30 minutes. Stir in the cream and transfer to a warm serving dish.

Cooking time: 45 to 50 minutes
Serves 4

Turkey Olives
(Photograph: British Turkey Federation)

Partridges in Red Wine

METRIC/IMPERIAL	AMERICAN
4 tablespoons oil	4 tablespoons oil
4 partridges, cleaned	4 partridges, cleaned
1 onion, chopped	1 onion, chopped
50 g/2 oz button mushrooms	½ cup button mushrooms
225 g/8 oz courgettes, sliced	½ lb zucchini, sliced
salt and pepper	salt and pepper
150 ml/¼ pint red wine	⅔ cup red wine
2 teaspoons plain flour	2 teaspoons all-purpose flour
2 tablespoons water	2 tablespoons water

Heat the oil in a pan and brown the partridges on all sides. Remove with a slotted spoon and drain on kitchen paper towels.

Add the onion, mushrooms and courgettes (zucchini) to the pan and sauté for 5 minutes. Remove with a slotted spoon and place in a large casserole dish. Arrange the partridges on top and sprinkle liberally with salt and pepper.

Pour the wine over, cover and cook in a preheated moderate oven (180°C/350°F, Gas Mark 4) for 1½ hours. Blend the flour with the water and stir into the juices. Continue to cook for 15 minutes, basting the partridges well. Serve hot.
Cooking time: 2 hours
Serves 4

Coq au Vin

METRIC/IMPERIAL	AMERICAN
2 tablespoons oil	2 tablespoons oil
25 g/1 oz butter	2 tablespoons butter
4 chicken joints	1 broiler, cut into 4 pieces
12 small onions, peeled	12 small onions, peeled
4 bacon rashers, chopped	4 bacon slices, chopped
100 g/4 oz button mushrooms	1 cup button mushrooms
300 ml/½ pint red wine	1¼ cups red wine
1 bouquet garni	1 bouquet garni
salt and pepper	salt and pepper
25 g/1 oz margarine	2 tablespoons margarine
2 tablespoons plain flour	2 tablespoons all-purpose flour

Heat the oil and butter in a large frying pan and cook the chicken for about 10 minutes until golden brown. Remove with a slotted spoon and place in a large casserole dish.

Add the onions, bacon and mushrooms to the pan and sauté for 5 minutes. Add to the casserole, then pour the wine over. Stir in the bouquet garni and salt and pepper to taste. Cook in a preheated moderate oven (180°C/ 350°F, Gas Mark 4) for 1½ hours.

Strain the juice from the casserole into a saucepan. Blend the margarine and flour together to make a beurre manié. Over a gentle heat, whisk small pieces into the wine juices. When the sauce has thickened, continue to cook, stirring, for 1 minute, then adjust the seasoning. Arrange the chicken and vegetables on a dish and pour the red wine sauce over.
Cooking time: 2 hours
Serves 4

Poussins Richelieu

METRIC/IMPERIAL	AMERICAN
4 poussins	4 poussins
Stuffing:	**Stuffing:**
25 g/1 oz butter	2 tablespoons butter
1 onion, chopped	1 onion, chopped
50 g/2 oz mushrooms, chopped	½ cup chopped mushrooms
100 g/4 oz ham pâté	¼ lb ham pâté
100 g/4 oz cooked ham, minced	½ cup ground cooked ham
2 tablespoons chopped parsley	2 tablespoons chopped parsley
grated rind and juice of 1 lemon	grated rind and juice of 1 lemon
50 g/2 oz fresh breadcrumbs	1 cup soft bread crumbs
salt and pepper	salt and pepper
1 egg, beaten	1 egg, beaten

To make the stuffing: melt the butter in a pan and sauté the onion and mushrooms gently for 5 minutes. Allow to cool, then add the pâté, ham, parsley, lemon rind, juice, crumbs, salt and pepper and egg to bind together.

Wash and dry the poussins and pack the stuffing in the neck cavities. Secure the skin with small skewers. Place the birds in a large roasting pan and dot with butter. Cook in a preheated moderate oven (180°C/350°F, Gas Mark 4) for 45 minutes until tender. Arrange on a platter and pour the juices over.
Cooking time: 55 minutes to 1 hour
Serves 4

Chicken Ragoût

METRIC/IMPERIAL	AMERICAN
25 g/1 oz butter	2 tablespoons butter
1 onion, sliced	1 onion, sliced
2 sticks celery, chopped	2 stalks celery, chopped
1 carrot, sliced	1 carrot, sliced
50 g/2 oz mushrooms, sliced	½ cup sliced mushrooms
300 ml/½ pint chicken stock	1¼ cups chicken stock or broth
1 bouquet garni	1 bouquet garni
salt and pepper	salt and pepper
1 tablespoon cornflour	1 tablespoon cornstarch
2 tablespoons sherry	2 tablespoons sherry
150 ml/¼ pint milk	⅔ cup milk
350 g/12 oz cooked chicken meat, chopped	1½ cups chopped cooked chicken meat
225 g/8 oz long grain rice, cooked	½ lb long grain rice, cooked
chopped parsley to garnish	chopped parsley for garnish

Melt the butter in a pan and sauté the onion, celery, carrot and mushrooms for 5 minutes. Add the stock, bouquet garni and salt and pepper to taste and bring to the boil. Cover and simmer for 20 minutes.

Blend the cornflour (cornstarch) with the sherry and stir into the vegetables with the milk. Heat, stirring, until the sauce thickens. Add the chicken and cover and simmer for 20 minutes. Remove the bouquet garni and adjust the seasoning. Arrange the cooked rice around the edge of a warm serving platter. Spoon the chicken ragoût into the centre and garnish with parsley.

Cooking time: 50 minutes
Serves 4

Chicken Véronique

METRIC/IMPERIAL	AMERICAN
1 × 1.5 kg/3½ lb roasting chicken	1 × 3½ lb roasting chicken
salt and pepper	salt and pepper
few sprigs of fresh herbs	few sprigs of fresh herbs
450 ml/¾ pint chicken stock	2 cups chicken stock or broth
50 g/2 oz butter	¼ cup butter
1 tablespoon cornflour	1 tablespoon cornstarch
2 tablespoons lemon juice	2 tablespoons lemon juice
2 tablespoons brandy	2 tablespoons brandy
6 tablespoons double cream	6 tablespoons heavy cream
175 g/6 oz white grapes, halved and seeded	1½ cups halved and pitted white grapes
parsley to garnish	parsley for garnish

Season inside the chicken with salt and pepper and add the herbs. Place in a roasting pan and pour around half the stock. Spread half the butter over the chicken and cover loosely with foil.

Cook in a preheated moderately hot oven (200°C/400°F, Gas Mark 6) for 1½ hours or until cooked through. Remove from the oven, carve into 6 portions and place on a serving dish. Keep hot.

Strain the pan juices into a saucepan. Blend together the remaining butter and cornflour (cornstarch), then gradually whisk into the pan juices over a gentle heat. When the sauce has thickened, add the lemon juice, brandy, and remaining stock. Heat, stirring, until the sauce thickens again.

Remove the sauce from the heat, stir in the cream and adjust the seasoning. Add the grapes and pour the sauce over the chicken pieces. Serve garnished with parsley.

Cooking time: 1¾ hours
Serves 6

Egg & Cheese Dishes

Ham Mousse

METRIC/IMPERIAL	AMERICAN
½ onion, peeled	½ onion, peeled
½ carrot, peeled	½ carrot, peeled
½ stick celery	½ stalk celery
1 bay leaf	1 bay leaf
3 peppercorns	3 peppercorns
300 ml/½ pint milk	1¼ cups milk
25 g/1 oz butter	2 tablespoons butter
25 g/1 oz plain flour	¼ cup flour
salt and pepper	salt and pepper
2 eggs, separated	2 eggs, separated
15 g/½ oz gelatine	1½ tablespoons unflavored gelatin
3 tablespoons water	3 tablespoons water
350 g/12 oz smoked ham, minced	1½ cups minced ham
3 tablespoons chopped parsley	3 tablespoons chopped parsley
2 teaspoons French mustard	2 teaspoons Dijon-style mustard
1 teaspoon tomato purée	1 teaspoon tomato paste
150 ml/¼ pint double cream	⅔ cup heavy cream
Garnish:	**Garnish:**
cucumber slices	cucumber slices
300 ml/½ pint aspic	1¼ cups aspic
parsley sprig	parsley sprig

Place the onion, carrot, celery, bay leaf and peppercorns in a pan with the milk. Gently bring to the boil, remove from the heat, cover and infuse for 15 minutes. Strain milk into a jug.

Melt the butter in a pan and stir in the flour. Cook for 1 minute and remove from the heat. Gradually blend in the strained milk. Return to the heat and cook, stirring, until sauce thickens. Add salt and pepper and beat in egg yolks.

Sprinkle the gelatine over the water in a heat-proof bowl and place over a pan of simmering water. Stir until dissolved. Cool the gelatine slightly then stir into the sauce with the ham, parsley, mustard and tomato purée (paste).

Whip the cream until thick and fold it into the ham mixture. Whisk the egg whites until stiff and fold in thoroughly. Adjust the seasoning, then pour the mixture into a 900 ml/1½ pint (5 cup) soufflé dish. Leave in refrigerator to set.

Arrange the cucumber on top and pour the aspic over. Chill until set. Garnish with parsley.
Cooking time: 15 to 20 minutes
Serves 6 to 8

Eggs Bayonnaise

METRIC/IMPERIAL	AMERICAN
6 tablespoons oil	6 tablespoons oil
8 small rounds bread	8 small rounds bread
8 eggs	8 eggs
225 g/8 oz bacon rashers	½ lb bacon slices
15 g/½ oz butter	1 tablespoon butter
350 g/12 oz button mushrooms	3 cups button mushrooms
salt and pepper	salt and pepper
2 teaspoons lemon juice	2 teaspoons lemon juice

Heat 4 tablespoons oil in a frying pan and fry the bread on both sides until golden. Drain on kitchen paper towels and keep hot. Add the remaining oil to the pan and fry the eggs. Place one egg on each bread round and keep hot.

Cut the bacon into strips. Melt the butter in the pan and cook the bacon for 5 minutes. Drain and keep hot. Add the mushrooms to the pan and sauté for 5 minutes, then add the salt and pepper to taste and lemon juice.

Place the eggs and bread on a warm serving platter with bacon between them and pile the mushrooms into the centre. Serve hot.
Cooking time: 20 to 25 minutes
Serves 4

Ham Mousse
(Photograph: Mattessons Meats)

French Omelette

METRIC/IMPERIAL	AMERICAN
3 eggs	3 eggs
1 tablespoon cold water	1 tablespoon cold water
salt and pepper	salt and pepper
15 g/½ oz butter	1 tablespoon butter

Place the eggs in a bowl with the water, salt and pepper. Lightly whisk with a fork to break up the whites and yolks.

Place an omelette pan over a moderate heat for 1 minute then add the butter. When the butter sizzles without becoming brown, pour in the egg mixture. Using a spatula, draw the cooked egg from the edge of the pan towards the centre so that the liquid egg runs through to cook on the bottom of the pan.

While the top of the omelette is still runny, fold over one-third of the omelette away from the pan handle. Add any filling (see suggestions below). Grip the handle underneath and shake the omelette to the edge of the pan. Tip over in three folds onto a warm serving platter. Serve immediately.
Cooking time: 5 to 10 minutes
Serves 1

Fillings for 1 serving:
25 g/1 oz (¼ cup) grated cheese
25 g/1 oz (2 tablespoons) chopped ham
50 g/2 oz (½ cup) chopped mushrooms, sautéed in butter
1 tablespoon chopped parsley
1 to 2 tablespoons chopped mixed herbs

Quiche Lorraine

METRIC/IMPERIAL	AMERICAN
100 g/4 oz plain flour	1 cup all-purpose flour
pinch of salt	pinch of salt
25 g/1 oz lard	2 tablespoons shortening
25 g/1 oz butter	2 tablespoons butter
1 tablespoon cold water	1 tablespoon cold water
Filling:	**Filling:**
100 g/4 oz lean bacon	¼ lb lean bacon slices
3 eggs	3 eggs
300 ml/½ pint single cream	1¼ cups light cream
salt and pepper	salt and pepper

Sift the flour and salt into a bowl. Rub (cut) in the lard (shortening) and butter until the mixture resembles fine breadcrumbs. Add the water and mix in with a knife, then knead the dough together with hands. Form into a smooth ball and turn onto a floured surface.

Roll out the dough and use to line a 20 cm/8 inch flan tin or dish (quiche pan), making sure there is no air trapped between the dough and the bottom of the tin (pan). Prick the bottom lightly with a fork and place the tin on a baking sheet. Cook in a preheated moderate oven (180°C/350°F, Gas Mark 4) for 15 minutes.

To make the filling: chop the bacon and cook in its own fat for 5 minutes. Drain on kitchen paper towels and arrange in the cooked pastry case (pie crust).

Beat the eggs and gradually add the cream and salt and pepper to taste. Pour over the bacon and return the quiche to the oven for 30 to 40 minutes or until risen and golden brown. Serve hot or cold.
Cooking time: 50 minutes to 1 hour
Serves 4

Pepper and Onion Quiche

METRIC/IMPERIAL	AMERICAN
1 × 20 cm/8 inch cooked pastry case (see page 36)	1 × 8 inch cooked pie crust (see page 36)
Filling:	**Filling:**
15 g/½ oz butter	1 tablespoon butter
1 small onion, finely chopped	1 small onion, finely chopped
½ green pepper, cored, seeded and sliced	½ green pepper, seeded and sliced
½ red pepper, cored, seeded and sliced	½ red pepper, seeded and sliced
3 eggs	3 eggs
300 ml/½ pint single cream	1¼ cups light cream
salt and pepper	salt and pepper

Melt the butter in a frying pan and sauté the onion and peppers until soft. Arrange in the pastry case (pie crust).

Beat the eggs and add the cream and salt and pepper to taste. Pour over the vegetables. Cook in a preheated moderate oven (180°C/350°F, Gas Mark 4) for 35 to 40 minutes or until well risen and golden. Serve hot or cold.
Cooking time: 40 to 45 minutes
Serves 4

Oeufs Florentine

METRIC/IMPERIAL	AMERICAN
4 eggs	4 eggs
450 g/1 lb spinach	1 lb spinach
15 g/½ oz butter	1 tablespoon butter
salt and pepper	salt and pepper
Sauce:	**Sauce:**
25 g/1 oz butter	2 tablespoons butter
25 g/1 oz plain flour	¼ cup all-purpose flour
300 ml/½ pint milk	1¼ cups milk
50 g/2 oz Cheddar cheese, grated	½ cup grated Cheddar cheese
¼ teaspoon mustard powder	¼ teaspoon mustard powder
salt and pepper	salt and pepper

Poach the eggs and leave in warm water until required.

Wash the spinach and remove the stalks. Cook until soft and drain well. Return the spinach to the pan with the butter and salt and pepper to taste. Heat gently for 1 to 2 minutes, then arrange the spinach along the centre of a greased, shallow flameproof dish. Place the eggs over the top.

To make the sauce: melt the butter in a pan and stir in the flour. Cook for 1 minute then remove from the heat. Gradually blend in the milk. Return the sauce to the heat and cook, stirring, until the sauce thickens. Stir in half the cheese, mustard and salt and pepper to taste. Pour the sauce over the eggs and sprinkle with the remaining cheese.

Cook under a preheated moderate grill (broiler) for 4 to 5 minutes. Serve immediately.
Cooking time: 25 minutes
Serves 4

Tomato and Anchovy Quiche

METRIC/IMPERIAL	AMERICAN
1 × 20 cm/8 inch cooked pastry case (see page 36)	1 × 8 inch cooked pie crust (see page 36)
Filling:	**Filling:**
1 × 397 g/14 oz can tomatoes	1 × 16 oz can tomatoes
1 onion, finely chopped	1 onion, finely chopped
1 clove garlic, crushed	1 clove garlic, crushed
1 teaspoon dried sage	1 teaspoon dried sage
2 eggs	2 eggs
150 ml/¼ pint beef stock	⅔ cup beef stock
salt and pepper	salt and pepper
Topping:	**Topping:**
1 × 50 g/1¾ oz can anchovy fillets, drained	1 × 1¾ oz can anchovy fillets, drained
black olives, halved and stoned	halved and pitted ripe olives

Drain the tomatoes and reserve the juice. Roughly chop the tomatoes and arrange in the pastry case (pie crust). Sprinkle with the onion, garlic and sage.

Beat the eggs and add the tomato juice, stock and salt and pepper to taste. Pour over the tomatoes and cook in a preheated moderate oven (180°C/350°F, Gas Mark 4) for 40 to 45 minutes or until set. Allow to cool.

Cut the anchovies in half lengthwise and arrange over the quiche. Place the olives between the anchovies.
Cooking time: 40 to 45 minutes
Serves 4

Courgette (Zucchini) and Garlic Quiche

METRIC/IMPERIAL

1 × 20 cm/8 inch
   cooked pastry case
   (see page 36)
Filling:
25 g/1 oz butter
225 g/8 oz courgettes,
   sliced
2 cloves garlic,
   crushed
50 g/2 oz garlic
   sausage, chopped
2 eggs
150 ml/¼ pint single
   cream
salt and pepper
50 g/2 oz Gruyère
   cheese, grated
Garnish:
garlic sausage slices,
   rolled into cones

AMERICAN

1 × 8 inch cooked pie
   crust (see page 36)
Filling:
2 tablespoons butter
½ lb zucchini, sliced
2 cloves garlic,
   crushed
¼ cup chopped garlic
   sausage
2 eggs
⅔ cup light cream
salt and pepper
½ cup grated Gruyère
   cheese
Garnish:
garlic sausage slices,
   rolled into cones

Melt the butter in a frying pan and sauté the courgettes (zucchini) and garlic until soft. Remove with a slotted spoon and arrange in the pastry case (pie crust). Sprinkle with the garlic sausage.

Beat the eggs and add the cream and salt and pepper to taste. Pour over the vegetables and sprinkle with the cheese. Cook in a preheated moderately hot oven (190°C/375°F, Gas Mark 5) for 30 to 40 minutes or until well risen and golden. Serve hot or cold garnished with cones of garlic sausage.
Cooking time: 35 to 45 minutes
Serves 4 to 6

Pipérade

METRIC/IMPERIAL

2 tablespoons oil
1 onion, thinly sliced
2 green peppers,
   cored, seeded and
   sliced
1 clove garlic,
   crushed
225 g/8 oz tomatoes,
   skinned and
   chopped
salt and pepper
6 eggs
4 rashers bacon

AMERICAN

2 tablespoons oil
1 onion, thinly sliced
2 green peppers,
   seeded and sliced
1 clove garlic,
   crushed
½ lb tomatoes,
   peeled and
   chopped
salt and pepper
6 eggs
4 bacon slices

Heat the oil in a large pan and sauté the onion until soft. Add the peppers and garlic and continue to cook for 5 minutes. Add the tomatoes and salt and pepper to taste; cover and cook for 20 minutes.

Lightly beat the eggs, pour into the vegetables and stir continuously until the eggs are just set.

While cooking the eggs, place the bacon under a preheated moderate grill (broiler) so that it is cooked when the eggs are ready.

Spoon the pipérade onto a warm, flat serving dish and arrange the bacon on top.
Cooking time: 35 to 40 minutes
Serves 4

Pipérade
(Photograph: British Egg Information Service)

Ham Gougère

METRIC/IMPERIAL	AMERICAN
Choux pastry:	**Choux paste:**
150 ml/¼ pint water	⅔ cup water
50 g/2 oz butter	¼ cup butter
65 g/2½ oz plain flour, sifted	⅔ cup all-purpose flour, sifted
pinch of salt	pinch of salt
2 eggs	2 eggs
50 g/2 oz Cheddar cheese, grated	½ cup grated Cheddar cheese
Filling:	**Filling:**
25 g/1 oz butter	2 tablespoons butter
2 onions, sliced	2 onions, sliced
50 g/2 oz mushrooms, sliced	½ cup sliced mushrooms
2 teaspoons plain flour	2 teaspoons all-purpose flour
150 ml/¼ pint stock	⅔ cup stock
3 tomatoes, skinned and quartered	3 tomatoes, peeled and quartered
100 g/4 oz cooked ham, chopped	½ cup chopped cooked ham
salt and pepper	salt and pepper
1 tablespoon grated Parmesan cheese	1 tablespoon grated Parmesan cheese
1 tablespoon browned breadcrumbs	1 tablespoon browned bread crumbs

Place the water and butter in a pan and heat until the butter melts and the water comes to the boil. Remove from the heat and quickly add all the flour and salt. Beat until the mixture is smooth and leaves the sides of the pan clean. Allow to cool.

Beat the eggs, then add a little at a time to the choux, beating well after each addition – the mixture should be stiff and glossy. Stir in the cheese and spread the mixture around the sides of a greased 23 cm/9 inch shallow ovenproof dish leaving a space in the centre.

To make the filling: melt the butter in a pan and sauté the onions for 5 minutes. Add the mushrooms and sauté for 1 minute. Blend in the flour and stock. Bring to the boil and simmer for 5 minutes.

Add the tomatoes, ham and salt and pepper to taste. Pour the filling into the middle of the choux ring. Mix together the Parmesan cheese and crumbs, then sprinkle over the top. Cook in a preheated moderately hot oven (200°C/400°F, Gas Mark 6) for 30 to 40 minutes or until well risen and golden. Serve hot.
Cooking time: 45 to 55 minutes
Serves 4

Ardennes Choux Balls

METRIC/IMPERIAL	AMERICAN
Choux balls:	**Choux balls:**
150 ml/¼ pint water	⅔ cup water
50 g/2 oz butter	¼ cup butter
65 g/2½ oz plain flour, sifted	⅔ cup sifted all-purpose flour
pinch of salt	pinch of salt
2 eggs	2 eggs
Filling:	**Filling:**
100 g/4 oz Ardennes pâté	¼ lb Ardennes pâté
50 g/2 oz cheese, finely grated	½ cup finely grated cheese
1 tablespoon chopped parsley	1 tablespoon chopped parsley
2 teaspoons chopped capers	2 teaspoons chopped capers
2 tablespoons brandy	2 tablespoons brandy
salt and pepper	salt and pepper
Topping:	**Topping:**
lightly whisked egg white	lightly whisked egg white
paprika pepper	paprika pepper
watercress to garnish	watercress for garnish

Place the water and butter in a pan and heat until the butter melts and the water comes to the boil. Remove from the heat and quickly add all the flour and salt. Beat until the mixture is smooth and leaves the sides of the pan clean. Allow to cool.

Beat the eggs, then add a little at a time to the paste, beating well after each addition – the mixture should be stiff and glossy.

Place teaspoonfuls of the mixture onto a greased baking sheet. Cook in a preheated moderately hot oven (200°C/400°F, Gas Mark 6) for 20 minutes. Remove from the oven and make a small slit in the side of each ball. Reduce the oven to moderate (180°C/350°F, Gas Mark 4) and return the choux balls for a further 10 minutes. Cool on a wire rack.

Mix together all the filling ingredients and use to fill the balls. Brush the tops with egg white and sprinkle with paprika pepper. Pile the balls onto a serving dish and garnish with watercress.
Cooking time: 35 minutes
Serves 4

Cheese and Onion Gratin

METRIC/IMPERIAL	AMERICAN
50 g/2 oz butter	¼ cup butter
225 g/8 oz onions, chopped	2 cups chopped onion
8 thin slices bread	8 thin slices bread
225 g/8 oz cheese, grated	2 cups grated cheese
2 eggs	2 eggs
salt and pepper	salt and pepper
150 ml/¼ pint single cream	⅔ cup light cream
300 ml/½ pint milk	1¼ cups milk
parsley sprigs to garnish	parsley sprigs for garnish

Melt the butter in a pan and sauté the onions for 5 minutes. Cut the bread into quarters and arrange half in a greased 1 litre/2 pint (1 quart) ovenproof dish. Sprinkle the onion and half the cheese over the bread, then arrange the remaining bread quarters neatly on top.

Beat together the eggs, salt and pepper, cream and milk. Pour over the bread and leave to soak for 30 minutes.

Sprinkle with the remaining cheese and cook in a preheated moderately hot oven (200°C/400°F, Gas Mark 6) for 30 to 40 minutes or until well risen and golden. Serve hot, garnished with parsley.
Cooking time: 30 to 40 minutes
Serves 4 to 6

Cheese Fondue

METRIC/IMPERIAL	AMERICAN
1 clove garlic, halved	1 clove garlic, halved
15 g/½ oz butter	1 tablespoon butter
300 ml/½ pint dry white wine	1¼ cups dry white wine
350 g/12 oz Cheddar cheese, coarsely grated	3 cups coarsely grated Cheddar cheese
1 tablespoon cornflour	1 tablespoon cornstarch
2 tablespoons brandy	2 tablespoons brandy
freshly ground black pepper	freshly ground black pepper
freshly grated nutmeg to taste	freshly grated nutmeg to taste
1 crusty French loaf, to serve	1 crusty French loaf, to serve

Rub the inside of a fondue dish, flameproof casserole or saucepan with the cut garlic clove. Add the butter and wine and heat until just beginning to bubble. Add the cheese and cook gently, stirring, until melted.

Blend the cornflour (cornstarch) with the brandy and stir into the fondue. Add pepper and nutmeg to taste. Cook gently for 3 to 5 minutes until smooth and creamy.

To serve, keep the fondue warm at the table by placing over a spirit burner. Cut the bread into cubes and place in a basket or serving dish. Provide long forks for each person to dip bread into the fondue. Serve with salads.
Cooking time: 10 to 15 minutes
Serves 4 to 6

Cheese Soufflé

METRIC/IMPERIAL	AMERICAN
50 g/2 oz butter	¼ cup butter
50 g/2 oz plain flour	½ cup all-purpose flour
300 ml/½ pint milk	1¼ cups milk
100 g/4 oz hard cheese, grated	1 cup grated cheese
salt and pepper	salt and pepper
¼ teaspoon mustard powder	¼ teaspoon mustard powder
3 eggs, separated	3 eggs, separated

Melt the butter in a heavy pan. Add the flour and cook for 1 minute. Remove from the heat and gradually blend in the milk. Return the sauce to the heat and cook, stirring, until the mixture thickens, then continue to cook for 1 minute. Stir in the cheese, salt and pepper to taste and mustard.

Add the egg yolks to the mixture and beat well. Whisk the egg whites until stiff but not dry. Fold 1 tablespoon into the cheese mixture then fold in the remainder. Spoon into an oiled 1 litre/2 pint (1 quart) soufflé dish. Cook in a preheated moderately hot oven (190°C/375°F, Gas Mark 5) for 35 to 45 minutes or until evenly brown and firm to the touch. Serve immediately with salad or green vegetables.
Cooking time: 40 to 50 minutes
Serves 4

Salads & Vegetable Dishes

Garlic Mushrooms

METRIC/IMPERIAL	AMERICAN
2-3 cloves garlic, crushed	2-3 cloves garlic, crushed
100 g/4 oz butter, softened	½ cup softened butter
salt and freshly ground black pepper	salt and freshly ground black pepper
1 tablespoon chopped parsley	1 tablespoon chopped parsley
24 mushrooms, stalks removed	24 mushrooms, stalks removed
a little extra melted butter	a little extra melted butter

Blend together the garlic, butter, salt and pepper to taste and the chopped parsley. Spoon the mixture into a piping (pastry) bag, fitted with a large piping nozzle.

Brush the mushrooms with a little melted butter and arrange on 4 individual ovenproof dishes. Pipe the garlic filling into each mushroom. Cook in a preheated moderately hot oven (200°C/400°F, Gas Mark 6) for 10 minutes. Serve very hot with crisp rolls or French bread.

Cooking time: 10 minutes
Serves 4

Garlic Mushrooms
(Photograph: Mushroom Growers' Association)

Chicory à la Française

METRIC/IMPERIAL	AMERICAN
8 heads chicory	8 heads endive
2 tablespoons lemon juice	2 tablespoons lemon juice
600 ml/1 pint water	2½ cups water
1 teaspoon salt	1 teaspoon salt
8 slices cooked ham	8 slices cooked ham
40 g/1½ oz butter	3 tablespoons butter
40 g/1½ oz plain flour	6 tablespoons all-purpose flour
600 ml/1 pint milk	2½ cups milk
100 g/4 oz hard cheese, grated	1 cup grated hard cheese
salt and pepper	salt and pepper
parsley to garnish	parsley for garnish

Core the chicory (endive) and remove damaged or bruised outside leaves. Place in a large pan and add the lemon juice, water and salt. Bring to the boil, reduce the heat and cover and simmer for 20 to 25 minutes or until the chicory (endive) is tender.

Drain thoroughly and wrap each head in a slice of ham. Arrange in a greased, shallow ovenproof dish.

Melt the butter in a pan, stir in the flour and cook for 1 minute. Remove from the heat and blend in the milk. Return the sauce to the heat and cook, stirring, until it thickens, then continue to cook for 1 minute. Add two-thirds of the cheese and salt and pepper to taste.

Pour the sauce over the ham rolls and sprinkle with the remaining cheese. Cook under a preheated moderate grill (broiler) for 5 minutes until golden brown. Serve hot, garnished with parsley.

Cooking time: 30 to 35 minutes
Serves 4 to 6

Mushroom Brochettes

METRIC/IMPERIAL	AMERICAN
Sauce:	**Sauce:**
12 egg yolks	12 egg yolks
4 tablespoons tarragon vinegar	¼ cup tarragon vinegar
2 teaspoons crushed black peppercorns	2 teaspoons crushed black peppercorns
6 tomatoes, skinned and chopped	6 tomatoes, peeled and chopped
1 teaspoon chopped parsley	1 teaspoon chopped parsley
¼ teaspoon dried tarragon	¼ teaspoon dried tarragon
1 bay leaf	1 bay leaf
juice of 2 lemons	juice of 2 lemons
450 g/1 lb butter, melted	2 cups melted butter
salt	salt
Stuffing:	**Stuffing:**
24 cup mushrooms	24 cup mushrooms
12 button mushrooms	12 button mushrooms
50 g/2 oz butter	¼ cup butter
1 onion, finely chopped	1 onion, finely chopped
1 clove garlic, crushed	1 clove garlic, crushed
40 g/1½ oz fresh breadcrumbs	¾ cup soft bread crumbs
salt and pepper	salt and pepper
1 egg, beaten	1 egg, beaten
Beer batter:	**Beer batter:**
90 g/3½ oz plain flour	⅞ cup all-purpose flour
salt	salt
120 ml/4 fl oz beer	½ cup beer
15 g/½ oz butter, melted	1 tablespoon melted butter
150 ml/¼ pint warm water	⅔ cup warm water
2 egg whites	2 egg whites
oil for deep fat frying	oil for deep fat frying

To make the sauce: place the egg yolks, vinegar, pepper, tomatoes, parsley and tarragon in a heatproof bowl. Place over a pan of hot water and beat until thickened. Add the bay leaf. Just before serving, beat in the lemon juice, melted butter and salt to taste.

To make the stuffing: remove the stalks from the cup mushrooms and chop finely with the button mushrooms. Melt the butter in a pan and sauté the onion for 5 minutes. Add the chopped mushrooms, garlic, breadcrumbs, salt and pepper. Mix well then bind together with the egg.

Divide the mixture between 12 of the cup mushrooms and cover with the remaining 12 to make ball shapes.

To make the batter: sift the flour and salt into a bowl. Make a well in the centre and add the beer. Beat until smooth. Stir in the melted butter and water to give a coating consistency. Whisk the egg whites until stiff and fold into the batter.

Dip the stuffed mushrooms into the batter and fry in the oil until golden brown and puffed up. Serve on skewers with the sauce.
Cooking time: 10 to 20 minutes
Serves 6 to 8

Avocado and Crab Gratiné

METRIC/IMPERIAL	AMERICAN
25 g/1 oz butter	2 tablespoons butter
1 onion, finely chopped	1 onion, finely chopped
2 sticks celery, chopped	2 stalks celery, chopped
1 tablespoon plain flour	1 tablespoon all-purpose flour
150 ml/¼ pint milk	⅔ cup milk
salt and pepper	salt and pepper
100 g/4 oz white crabmeat	¼ lb white crab meat
2 tablespoons plain yogurt	2 tablespoons plain yogurt
2 avocados	2 avocados
lemon juice	lemon juice
50 g/2 oz fresh breadcrumbs	1 cup soft bread crumbs

Melt the butter and sauté the onion and celery for 5 minutes. Add the flour and cook for 1 minute. Remove from the heat and gradually blend in the milk. Return the sauce to the heat and cook, stirring, until the sauce thickens, then continue to cook for 1 to 2 minutes. Cool slightly. Stir in the salt and pepper to taste, crabmeat and yogurt and mix well.

Cut the avocados in half and remove the stones (seeds). Brush the cut surfaces with lemon juice. Spoon the crab mixture into the centre of the avocados and sprinkle with breadcrumbs.

Arrange the avocados in a shallow ovenproof dish and cook in a preheated moderately hot oven (200°C/400°F, Gas Mark 6) for 10 to 15 minutes or until the crumbs are browned. Serve with a green salad.
Cooking time: 20 to 25 minutes
Serves 4

Stuffed Courgettes (Zucchini)

METRIC/IMPERIAL	AMERICAN
4 large courgettes	4 large zucchini
salt and pepper	salt and pepper
½ inch thick slice of bread	½ inch thick slice of bread
water	water
3 tablespoons oil	3 tablespoons oil
1 onion, finely chopped	1 onion, finely chopped
3 tomatoes, skinned and chopped	3 tomatoes, peeled and chopped
1 clove garlic, crushed	1 clove garlic, crushed

Cut the courgettes (zucchini) in half lengthwise and scoop out the flesh with a teaspoon. Cook the shells in boiling salted water for 5 minutes and drain well. Soak the bread in a little water. Chop the courgette (zucchini) flesh. Heat 2 tablespoons oil in a frying pan and sauté the flesh with the onion for 5 minutes. Stir in the tomatoes and garlic. Squeeze the water from the bread and add the bread to the mixture. Stir and add salt and pepper to taste.

Divide the mixture between the courgette (zucchini) halves and arrange in a greased, shallow ovenproof dish. Spoon over the remaining oil, cover with foil and cook in a preheated moderately hot oven (190°C/375°F, Gas Mark 5) for 15 minutes. Remove the foil and cook for a further 15 minutes. Serve hot.
Cooking time: 40 minutes
Serves 4

Ratatouille

METRIC/IMPERIAL	AMERICAN
1 medium aubergine	1 medium eggplant
salt	salt
3 tablespoons oil	3 tablespoons oil
1 large onion, sliced	1 large onion, sliced
1 green pepper, cored, seeded and sliced	1 green pepper, seeded and sliced
450 g/1 lb tomatoes, skinned and sliced	1 lb tomatoes, peeled and sliced
450 g/1 lb courgettes, sliced	1 lb zucchini, sliced
½ teaspoon dried basil	½ teaspoon dried basil
1 clove garlic, crushed	1 clove garlic, crushed
pepper	pepper

Slice the aubergine (eggplant) and sprinkle with salt. Leave for 1 hour then rinse, drain and dry on kitchen paper towels.

Heat the oil in a large pan and sauté the aubergine (eggplant) and onion for 5 minutes. Add the green pepper, tomatoes and courgettes (zucchini). Bring to the boil, add the basil, garlic and salt and pepper to taste. Cover and simmer for 40 to 50 minutes. Transfer to a serving dish and serve hot or cold.
Cooking time: 50 minutes to 1 hour
Serves 4 to 6

Asparagus and Prawn Gratin

METRIC/IMPERIAL	AMERICAN
450 g/1 lb young asparagus, trimmed	1 lb young asparagus, trimmed
salt and pepper	salt and pepper
25 g/1 oz butter	2 tablespoons butter
50 g/2 oz button mushrooms, quartered	½ cup quartered button mushrooms
50 g/2 oz peeled prawns, chopped	⅓ cup chopped shelled shrimp
3 tablespoons single cream	3 tablespoons light cream
50 g/2 oz Cheddar cheese, grated	½ cup grated Cheddar cheese
25 g/1 oz grated Parmesan cheese	¼ cup grated Parmesan cheese

Tie the asparagus in bundles of 6 to 8 stalks. Stand upright in a pan of boiling salted water and cook for 10 minutes or until tender. Drain well, remove ties and place asparagus in a shallow ovenproof dish.

Melt the butter in a pan and sauté the mushrooms for 5 minutes. Remove from the heat and stir in the prawns (shrimp), cream and salt and pepper to taste. Pour this mixture over the asparagus.

Mix the cheeses together and sprinkle over the asparagus. Cook under a preheated moderate grill (broiler) for 10 minutes or until the top is golden brown.
Cooking time: 25 to 35 minutes
Serves 4

Spinach Ramekins

METRIC/IMPERIAL
25 g/1 oz butter
1 small onion,
  chopped
4 tablespoons
  spinach purée
50 g/2 oz Edam
  cheese, grated
4 eggs, beaten
pinch of nutmeg
salt and pepper
300 ml/½ pint milk
50 g/2 oz fresh
  breadcrumbs

AMERICAN
2 tablespoons butter
1 small onion,
  chopped
4 tablespoons
  spinach purée
½ cup grated Edam
  cheese
4 eggs, beaten
pinch of nutmeg
salt and pepper
1¼ cups milk
1 cup soft bread
  crumbs

Melt the butter in a pan and sauté the onion until soft, then place in a bowl with the spinach, cheese, eggs, nutmeg and salt and pepper to taste.

Heat the milk until almost boiling and beat into the mixture with the breadcrumbs. Pour into 4 greased ramekin dishes. Stand the ramekins in a roasting pan and half fill with water. Cook in a preheated moderate oven (180°C/350°F, Gas Mark 4) for 30 to 35 minutes or until risen and firm to the touch. Serve hot.
Cooking time: 35 to 40 minutes
Serves 4

Tomatoes au Fromage

METRIC/IMPERIAL
4 large ripe tomatoes
Filling:
25 g/1 oz butter
1 small onion, finely
  chopped
50 g/2 oz streaky
  bacon, chopped
50 g/2 oz fresh
  breadcrumbs
1 tablespoon chopped
  parsley
salt and pepper
50 g/2 oz Cheddar
  cheese, grated
Sauce:
15 g/½ oz butter
15 g/½ oz plain flour
150 ml/¼ pint milk
50 g/2 oz Cheddar
  cheese, grated
1 teaspoon made
  mustard
salt and pepper
Topping:
25 g/1 oz fresh
  breadcrumbs

AMERICAN
4 large ripe tomatoes
Filling:
2 tablespoons butter
1 small onion, finely
  chopped
¼ cup chopped fatty
  bacon
1 cup soft bread
  crumbs
1 tablespoon chopped
  parsley
salt and pepper
½ cup grated
  Cheddar cheese
Sauce:
1 tablespoon butter
2 tablespoons
  all-purpose flour
⅔ cup milk
½ cup grated
  Cheddar cheese
1 teaspoon prepared
  mustard
salt and pepper
Topping:
½ cup soft bread
  crumbs

Cut the tops from the tomatoes and scoop out the centres with a teaspoon.

To make the filling: melt the butter in a pan and sauté the onion and bacon until brown. Add the breadcrumbs, parsley, salt and pepper to taste and cheese. Mix well and spoon the mixture into the tomatoes.

To make the sauce: melt the butter in a pan, stir in the flour and cook for 1 minute. Remove from the heat and blend in the milk. Return the sauce to the heat and cook, stirring, until the sauce thickens. Stir in the cheese, mustard and salt and pepper to taste. Spoon a little sauce over each tomato and sprinkle with the breadcrumbs.

Place under a preheated moderate grill (broiler) for 5 minutes or until golden brown. Serve hot.
Cooking time: 15 minutes
Serves 4

Spinach Ramekins
(Photograph: Outline Slimming Bureau)

Pissaladière

METRIC/IMPERIAL	AMERICAN
Base:	**Base:**
350 g/12 oz	3 cups self-rising flour
self-raising flour	½ teaspoon salt
½ teaspoon salt	6 tablespoons butter
75 g/3 oz butter	⅔ cup milk
150 ml/¼ pint milk	**Topping:**
Topping:	2 lb large onions
1 kg/2 lb large onions	4 tablespoons oil
4 tablespoons oil	1 × 16 oz can
1 × 397 g/14 oz can	tomatoes, drained
tomatoes, drained	1 clove garlic,
1 clove garlic,	crushed
crushed	salt and pepper
salt and pepper	**Garnish:**
Garnish:	1 × 2½ oz can
1 × 56 g/2½ oz can	anchovies, drained
anchovies, drained	pitted ripe olives
black olives, stoned	

To make the base: sift the flour and salt into a bowl. Rub (cut) in the butter until the mixture resembles fine breadcrumbs. Add the milk and bind to a soft dough. Turn onto a floured surface and knead until smooth. Roll out the dough to a rectangle to line a greased baking sheet 18 × 28 cm (7 × 11 inches).

To make the topping: thinly slice the onions. Heat the oil in a pan and sauté the onions for 5 minutes. Cover the pan and cook gently for 30 minutes or until the onions are really soft. Stir in the tomatoes, garlic and salt and pepper to taste. Continue to cook for 10 minutes.

Spread the topping mixture over the dough base. Cut the anchovy fillets lengthwise and arrange in a lattice design over the onion mixture. Cook in a preheated hot oven (220°C/425°F, Gas Mark 7) for 30 minutes. Arrange olives on top. Serve hot.
Cooking time: 1¼ hours
Serves 4 to 6

Potatoes Lyonnaise

METRIC/IMPERIAL	AMERICAN
750 g/1½ lb potatoes	1½ lb potatoes
2 onions	2 onions
40 g/1½ oz butter	3 tablespoons butter
salt and pepper	salt and pepper
Garnish:	**Garnish:**
chopped parsley	chopped parsley
chopped chives	chopped chives

Blanch the potatoes in boiling water for 1 minute, then drain. Thinly slice the onions. Melt the butter in a pan and sauté the onions for 5 minutes.

Slice the potatoes thinly then layer them with the onions, salt and pepper in a greased 1 litre/2 pint (1 quart) casserole dish, finishing with potatoes. Cover the casserole.

Cook in a preheated moderately hot oven (200°C/400°F, Gas Mark 6) for 1 hour. Remove the lid and continue to cook for 30 minutes to allow the potatoes to brown.

Mix together the parsley and chives and sprinkle over the potatoes before serving.
Cooking time: 1 hour 35 minutes
Serves 4

Salade Niçoise

METRIC/IMPERIAL	AMERICAN
225 g/8 oz cooked	½ lb cooked new
new potatoes	potatoes
2 tomatoes, skinned	2 tomatoes, peeled
and quartered	and quartered
2 hard-boiled eggs,	2 hard-cooked eggs,
quartered	quartered
350 g/12 oz French	1½ cups cooked
beans, cooked	green beans
50 g/2 oz black olives,	⅓ cup pitted ripe
stoned	olives
1 × 198 g/7 oz can	1 × 7 oz can tuna fish,
tuna fish, drained	drained and flaked
and flaked	4 anchovy fillets
4 anchovy fillets	3 tablespoons French
3 tablespoons French	dressing
dressing	chopped parsley for
chopped parsley to	garnish
garnish	

Cut the potatoes into dice and arrange around the edge of a serving platter.

Toss together the tomatoes, eggs, beans, olives and tuna fish. Pile into the centre of the dish. Cut the anchovies lengthwise and arrange in a lattice pattern over the salad. Pour the dressing over and garnish with parsley. Serve with crusty bread.
Serves 4

Aubergine (Eggplant) and Carrot Terrine

METRIC/IMPERIAL	AMERICAN
Aubergine layer:	**Eggplant layer:**
2 medium aubergines	2 medium eggplants
salt and pepper	salt and pepper
25 g/1 oz butter	2 tablespoons butter
1 tablespoon plain flour	1 tablespoon all-purpose flour
3 eggs, separated	3 eggs, separated
150 ml/¼ pint plain yogurt	⅔ cup plain yogurt
75 g/3 oz cheese, grated	¾ cup grated cheese
Carrot layer:	**Carrot layer:**
5 medium carrots	5 medium carrots
salt and pepper	salt and pepper
1 teaspoon soft brown sugar	1 teaspoon soft brown sugar
3 eggs, separated	3 eggs, separated
150 ml/¼ pint plain yogurt	⅔ cup plain yogurt
75 g/3 oz cheese, grated	¾ cup grated cheese

Slice the aubergines (eggplants), sprinkle with salt and leave for 2 hours. Rinse under cold water and cut each slice into 4 pieces. Melt the butter in a pan and sauté the aubergines (eggplants) for 5 to 10 minutes or until very soft. Add the flour and blend well. Continue to cook for 5 minutes.

Remove the aubergines (eggplants) from the heat, cool, then add the egg yolks, yogurt, salt and pepper to taste and cheese. Mix well and leave on one side.

To make the carrot layer: peel and slice the carrots, then cook in boiling water until soft. Drain well and add salt and pepper to taste and sugar. Mash the carrots until smooth, then stir in the egg yolks, yogurt and cheese. Mix well.

Whisk the six egg whites until stiff and add half to the aubergine (eggplant) mixture and half to the carrot mixture. Fold in gently and adjust the seasoning.

Fill a greased 1.5 litre/2½ pint (1½ quart) terrine or soufflé dish with alternate layers of the mixtures. Cook in a preheated moderately hot oven (190°C/375°F, Gas Mark 5) for 30 to 40 minutes or until set. Allow to cool, invert onto a platter and cut into slices to serve.
Cooking time: 55 minutes to 1 hour 10 minutes
Serves 4 to 6

Salade Antiboise

METRIC/IMPERIAL	AMERICAN
750 g/1½ lb cod fillets	1½ lb cod fillets
2 tablespoons lemon juice	2 tablespoons lemon juice
2 tablespoons white wine vinegar	2 tablespoons white wine vinegar
6 tablespoons oil	6 tablespoons oil
¼ teaspoon dried tarragon	¼ teaspoon dried tarragon
salt and pepper	salt and pepper
225 g/8 oz cooked new potatoes, quartered	½ lb cooked new potatoes, quartered
100 g/4 oz pickled beetroot, diced	¼ lb pickled beet, diced
½ cucumber, diced	½ cucumber, diced
anchovy fillets to garnish	anchovy fillets for garnish

Skin the cod fillets and place on a foil-lined grill (broiler) pan.

Place the lemon juice, vinegar, oil, tarragon and salt and pepper in a screw top jar and shake vigorously until the ingredients are well blended. Brush some of the dressing over the fish, then grill (broil) for 10 minutes, turning once and brushing with the dressing. Allow to cool.

Cut the fish into pieces and combine with the potatoes, beetroot and cucumber. Pour over the remaining dressing, mix well and adjust the seasoning. Spoon on to a serving dish and garnish with the anchovy fillets arranged in a criss-cross pattern.
Cooking time: 10 to 15 minutes
Serves 4

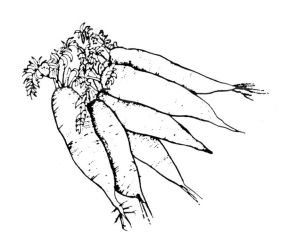

Gâteaux & Desserts

Gâteau Diane

METRIC/IMPERIAL	AMERICAN
Meringue:	**Meringue:**
3 egg whites	3 egg whites
175 g/6 oz sugar	¾ cup sugar
2 teaspoons coffee	2 teaspoons coffee
powder	powder
Buttercream:	**Buttercream:**
175 g/6 oz unsalted	¾ cup unsalted butter
butter	3 egg yolks
3 egg yolks	¾ cup sugar
175 g/6 oz granulated	¼ cup water
sugar	5 squares (1 oz each)
4 tablespoons water	semi-sweet
150 g/5 oz plain	chocolate, melted
chocolate, melted	**Decoration:**
Decoration:	½ cup toasted
50 g/2 oz flaked	slivered almonds
almonds, toasted	confectioners' sugar
icing sugar	

Line 2 baking sheets with non-stick (parchment) paper. Mark three 15 cm/6 inch circles on the paper.

Whisk the egg whites until stiff, then whisk in half the sugar. Fold in the remaining sugar with the coffee. Pipe or spread the meringue over the 3 circles. Cook in a preheated very cool oven (110°C/225°F, Gas Mark ¼) for 4 hours. They may be turned over for the last hour. When cold, store in an airtight container.

To make the filling: cream the butter until soft. In a separate bowl, beat the egg yolks until pale. Place the sugar and water in a pan and heat gently until the sugar has dissolved, then boil rapidly until the short thread stage is reached – 102°C/216°F on a sugar thermometer.

Gâteau Diane
(Photograph: Cadbury Typhoo Food Advisory Service)

Beat the syrup into the egg yolks and continue beating, adding the butter. Stir in the melted chocolate and leave to cool and thicken.

Assemble the gâteau by sandwiching the meringues with the chocolate filling. Spread the remainder over the top and sides. Press on the almonds. Lay 3 strips of paper across the top of the gâteau and dust with sifted icing (confectioners') sugar. Serve on a platter.
Cooking time: about 4 hours
Serves 6 to 8

Crème Brûlée

METRIC/IMPERIAL	AMERICAN
600 ml/1 pint double	2½ cups heavy cream
cream	1 vanilla bean
1 vanilla pod	6 egg yolks
6 egg yolks	3 tablespoons sugar
3 tablespoons caster	
sugar	

Place the cream and vanilla pod (bean) in a pan and heat very gently to just below boiling point. Beat the egg yolks with 1 tablespoon sugar until pale in colour.

Remove the vanilla pod (bean) from the cream, then stir the cream into the egg mixture and mix well. Pour into 6 greased ramekin dishes. Stand them in a roasting pan half filled with warm water. Cook in a preheated moderate oven (160°C/325°F, Gas Mark 3) for 20 to 25 minutes. Leave until cold, preferably in the refrigerator overnight.

Sprinkle the remaining sugar over the custards and place under a preheated moderate grill (broiler) until an even coating of caramel forms. Cool and place in the refrigerator for 2 to 3 hours before serving.
Cooking time: 35 to 40 minutes
Serves 6

Soufflé Milanaise

METRIC/IMPERIAL	AMERICAN
15 g/½ oz gelatine	1½ tablespoons unflavored gelatin
3 tablespoons water	3 tablespoons water
finely grated rind and juice of 2 lemons	finely grated rind and juice of 2 lemons
4 eggs, separated	4 eggs, separated
100 g/4 oz caster sugar	½ cup sugar
150 ml/¼ pint double cream	⅔ cup heavy cream
50 g/2 oz almonds, chopped and toasted	½ cup chopped toasted almonds

Prepare a 600 ml/1 pint (2½ cup) soufflé dish by tying a double band of greaseproof (waxed) paper around the dish to come 7.5 cm/3 inches above rim. Brush dish and paper with oil.

Sprinkle the gelatine over the water in a heatproof bowl. Place over a pan of simmering water and stir until gelatine has dissolved.

Place the lemon rind and juice in a bowl with the egg yolks and sugar. Whisk until thick and pale in colour. Pour in the gelatine in a steady stream, whisking continuously.

Whip the cream until thick and fold into the lemon mixture. Whisk the egg whites until stiff and fold in evenly. Pour into the prepared soufflé dish and leave to set.

Carefully remove the paper collar and press the almonds to the sides of the soufflé. Serve chilled and decorated with cream if liked.
Serves 6

Magda

METRIC/IMPERIAL	AMERICAN
225 g/8 oz plain chocolate	8 squares (1 oz each) semi-sweet chocolate
1 tablespoon coffee powder	1 tablespoon coffee powder
1 teaspoon vanilla essence	1 teaspoon vanilla
300 ml/½ pint boiling water	1¼ cups boiling water
15 g/½ oz gelatine	1½ tablespoons unflavored gelatin
3 tablespoons water	3 tablespoons water
150 ml/¼ pint double cream	⅔ cup heavy cream
crystallized rose petals to decorate	crystallized rose petals to decorate
4 sponge fingers	4 lady fingers

Break the chocolate into pieces and place in a pan with the coffee and vanilla. Pour over the boiling water and whisk over a gentle heat until the chocolate has melted.

Sprinkle the gelatine over the water in a heatproof bowl. Place over a pan of gently simmering water and stir until dissolved. Cool slightly and stir into the chocolate mixture. Leave until beginning to thicken.

Whip the cream until thick and reserve a little for decoration. Fold the remainder into the chocolate mixture. Divide between 4 glass dishes and leave to set.

Decorate with cream and rose petals and serve chilled with sponge (lady) fingers.
Cooking time: 10 minutes
Serves 4

Chocolate Bavarois

METRIC/IMPERIAL	AMERICAN
3 eggs	3 eggs
2 teaspoons cornflour	2 teaspoons cornstarch
2 tablespoons caster sugar	2 tablespoons sugar
½ teaspoon vanilla essence	½ teaspoon vanilla
450 ml/¾ pint milk	2 cups milk
100 g/4 oz plain chocolate, melted	4 squares (1 oz each) semi-sweet chocolate, melted
20 g/¾ oz gelatine	2½ tablespoons unflavored gelatin
4 tablespoons water	4 tablespoons water
150 ml/¼ pint double cream	⅔ cup heavy cream
whipped cream to decorate	whipped cream for decoration

Place the eggs, cornflour (cornstarch) and sugar in a bowl and whisk until pale. Add the vanilla. Heat the milk until almost boiling, then stir in the chocolate. Pour onto the egg mixture, blend well and return to the pan. Cook, stirring continuously, until the custard coats the back of the spoon. Strain into a bowl to cool.

Sprinkle the gelatine over the water in a heatproof bowl. Place over a pan of gently simmering water and stir until dissolved. Allow to cool, then whisk into the custard. Whip the cream until thick and fold in with a metal spoon. Spoon the mixture into an oiled 900 ml/ 1½ pint (5 cup) plain mould. Leave in a cool place to set.

Invert carefully onto a serving platter and decorate with whirls of whipped cream.
Cooking time: 5 to 10 minutes
Serves 6

Paris Brest

METRIC/IMPERIAL	AMERICAN
Choux ring:	**Choux ring:**
150 ml/¼ pint water	⅔ cup water
50 g/2 oz butter	¼ cup butter
65 g/2½ oz plain flour, sifted	⅔ cup all-purpose flour, sifted
pinch of salt	pinch of salt
2 eggs, beaten	2 eggs, beaten
Topping:	**Topping:**
½ beaten egg	½ beaten egg
½ teaspoon water	½ teaspoon water
1 tablespoon flaked almonds	1 tablespoon slivered almonds
Crème pâtissière:	**Crème pâtissière:**
1 egg	1 egg
1 egg yolk	1 egg yolk
50 g/2 oz caster sugar	¼ cup sugar
40 g/1½ oz plain flour	⅓ cup all-purpose flour
300 ml/½ pint milk	1¼ cups milk

To make the choux ring: place the water and butter in a pan. Heat until the butter melts and the liquid is boiling. Remove from the heat and quickly add all the flour and salt. Beat until smooth and the mixture leaves the sides of the pan. Allow to cool.

Gradually beat in the eggs, a little at a time. The mixture should look smooth and glossy. Spoon into a piping (pastry) bag fitted with a plain 2.5 cm/1 inch nozzle. Pipe a 20 cm/8 inch ring onto a greased baking sheet.

For the topping: mix the egg and water and brush over the choux ring with a pastry brush. Sprinkle with the almonds. Cook in a preheated moderately hot oven (200°C/400°F, Gas Mark 6) for 30 to 35 minutes or until the choux is puffed and golden brown. Remove from the oven and using a sharp knife make a shallow horizontal slit around the ring. Turn off oven and replace ring for 10 minutes. Cool on a wire rack.

To make the crème pâtissière: beat together the egg, egg yolk and sugar until thick and pale. Blend the flour with a little milk and stir into the eggs. Heat the remaining milk until almost boiling then stir into the egg mixture. Return to the pan and heat, stirring continuously, until the mixture thickens. Spoon into a bowl to cool. Cover to prevent a skin forming.

Carefully cut the choux ring in half horizontally and place one half on a serving platter. Cover with the crème pâtissière and place the almond covered half on top.
Cooking time: 45 to 50 minutes
Serves 6

Soufflé Glacé au Fine Champagne

METRIC/IMPERIAL	AMERICAN
300 ml/½ pint double cream	1¼ cups heavy cream
3 tablespoons brandy	3 tablespoons brandy
5 tablespoons champagne*	5 tablespoons champagne*
finely grated rind and juice of ½ lemon	finely grated rind and juice of ½ lemon
4 eggs, separated	4 eggs, separated
75 g/3 oz caster sugar	⅓ cup sugar
Decoration:	**Decoration:**
whipped cream	whipped cream
grapes	grapes

Tie a band of foil round the outside of a 900 ml/ 1½ pint (5 cup) soufflé dish to stand 5 cm/ 2 inches above the rim.

Place the cream, brandy, champagne, lemon rind and juice in a bowl and whip until softly stiff. Whisk the egg yolks and sugar together until thick and foamy, then fold into the cream.

Whisk the egg whites until stiff and fold into the mixture evenly. Spoon into the soufflé dish, smooth the top and place in a freezer until firm.

Remove the soufflé from the freezer and carefully remove the foil band. Decorate with whipped cream and grapes.

Leave the soufflé at room temperature for 15 to 20 minutes before serving.
Serves 8
***Note:** white wine can be used in place of the champagne.

Red Berry Salad

METRIC/IMPERIAL	AMERICAN
450 ml/¾ pint water	2 cups water
175 g/6 oz caster sugar	¾ cup sugar
225 g/8 oz fresh redcurrants, stalks removed	2 cups fresh redcurrants, stalks removed
450 g/1 lb strawberries, hulled	3 cups strawberries, hulled
225 g/8 oz raspberries	1½ cups raspberries

Place the water. and sugar in a pan and heat gently to dissolve the sugar, then boil for 3 minutes. Remove from the heat and allow to cool for 5 minutes. Stir in the redcurrants and leave until quite cold. Add the strawberries and raspberries. Spoon into a bowl and chill. Serve with cream.
Serves 6

Blackcurrant Sorbet

METRIC/IMPERIAL	AMERICAN
225 g/8 oz fresh blackcurrants	2 cups fresh blackcurrants
300 ml/½ pint water	1¼ cups water
100 g/4 oz granulated sugar	½ cup sugar
1 teaspoon lemon juice	1 teaspoon lemon juice
2 egg whites	2 egg whites

Place the blackcurrants in a pan with 1 tablespoon water and cook gently until the fruit is soft. Sieve or place the fruit in a blender or food processor to make a purée. If necessary make up to 600 ml/1 pint (2½ cups) with water.

Place the remaining water and sugar in a pan. Heat gently to dissolve the sugar, then boil for 10 minutes. Allow to cool.

Mix together the blackcurrant purée, syrup and lemon juice. Pour into a shallow container and freeze for 1 hour.

Place the frozen mixture into a chilled bowl and break down with a fork. Whisk the egg whites until stiff and fold into the fruit. Return to the tray and freeze until firm.

To serve, leave the sorbet in the refrigerator for 20 minutes, then spoon into glass dishes.
Cooking time: 20 minutes
Serves 4 to 6

Tarte aux Cerises

METRIC/IMPERIAL	AMERICAN
Pastry:	**Dough:**
75 g/3 oz butter	6 tablespoons butter
50 g/2 oz caster sugar	¼ cup sugar
1 egg yolk	1 egg yolk
150 g/5 oz plain flour	1¼ cups all-purpose flour
Filling:	**Filling:**
300 ml/½ pint double cream	1¼ cups heavy cream
40 g/1½ oz ratafias, crushed	½ cup crushed ratafias
½ teaspoon almond essence	½ teaspoon almond extract
Topping:	**Topping:**
450 g/1 lb red cherries, stoned	1 lb pitted red cherries
3 tablespoons redcurrant jelly	3 tablespoons red currant jelly
1 tablespoon water or cherry brandy	1 tablespoon water or cherry brandy

To make the pastry: place the butter, sugar, egg yolk and flour in a bowl and knead together. Chill for 10 to 15 minutes then roll out and line a 20 cm/8 inch fluted dish or ring. Lightly prick the bottom and cook in a preheated moderate oven (180°C/350°F, Gas Mark 4) for 15 to 20 minutes. Allow to cool.

Whip the cream until stiff and fold in the ratafias and almond essence (extract). Spoon into the pastry case (pie crust).

Arrange the cherries on top of the cream. Place the redcurrant jelly in a pan with the water or cherry brandy. Heat gently then brush over the cherries as a glaze.
Cooking time: 15 to 20 minutes
Serves 4 to 6

Red Berry Salad; Tarte aux Cerises
(Photograph: British Sugar Bureau)

Breton Apple and Lemon Crêpes

METRIC/IMPERIAL	AMERICAN
Crêpes:	**Crêpes:**
100 g/4 oz plain flour	1 cup all-purpose flour
pinch of salt	pinch of salt
1 egg	1 egg
300 ml/½ pint milk	1¼ cups milk
oil for frying	oil for frying
Filling:	**Filling:**
450 g/1 lb apples, peeled, cored and sliced	1 lb apples, peeled, cored and sliced
75 g/3 oz soft brown sugar	½ cup light brown sugar
1 tablespoon water	1 tablespoon water
1 tablespoon lemon juice	1 tablespoon lemon juice
2 teaspoons finely grated lemon rind	2 teaspoons finely grated lemon rind
2 tablespoons Calvados	2 tablespoons applejack
whipped cream to serve	whipped cream to serve

Sift the flour and salt into a bowl and make a well in the centre. Add the egg and half the milk, then beat until smooth. Gradually blend in the remaining milk. Pour into a jug.

Heat an 18 cm/7 inch frying pan and brush with oil. Pour in enough batter to cover the bottom. Cook over a medium heat until the underside is golden. Toss or turn the crêpe and cook the other side. Make seven more crêpes. Keep them warm by stacking, interleaved with greaseproof (waxed) paper, on a plate over a pan of hot water.

To make the filling: place the apples, sugar, water, lemon juice and rind in a pan. Cook gently, covered, for 15 minutes or until the apples are soft.

Layer the crêpes and apples in a shallow serving dish, finishing with a crêpe. Pour over the Calvados (applejack) and serve cut in wedges with whipped cream.
Cooking time: 30 minutes
Serves 4 to 6

Fruit Brioche

METRIC/IMPERIAL	AMERICAN
500 g/1¼ lb strong plain flour	5 cups strong all-purpose flour
½ teaspoon salt	½ teaspoon salt
25 g/1 oz fresh yeast	1 cake compressed yeast
1 tablespoon sugar	1 tablespoon sugar
9 tablespoons warm water	9 tablespoons warm water
100 g/4 oz butter, melted	½ cup melted butter
2 eggs, beaten	2 eggs, beaten
100 g/4 oz sultanas	¾ cup golden raisins
beaten egg to glaze	beaten egg to glaze

Oil a 23 cm/9 inch brioche dish or tin (pan).

Sift the flour and salt into a bowl. Cream together the yeast, sugar, water and butter. Blend in the eggs and add to the flour. Mix to a soft dough then place on a floured surface. Knead lightly for 5 minutes then place in an oiled polythene bag. Leave in a warm place until the dough has doubled in size.

Knock back (punch down) the dough and knead well for 10 minutes, incorporating the sultanas (raisins). Reserve a quarter of the dough for the knob and place the remainder in the dish or tin (pan). Knead the reserved dough into a neat round and place on top.

Leave the brioche in a warm place until it rises to the top of the dish or tin (pan). Brush with beaten egg and cook in a preheated hot oven (220°C/425°F, Gas Mark 7) for 10 minutes.

Reduce the temperature to 190°C/375°F, Gas Mark 5 and cook brioche for 30 minutes. Invert onto wire rack and serve while still slightly warm
Cooking time: 35 to 40 minutes
Serves 8 to 10

Strawberry Gâteau

METRIC/IMPERIAL	AMERICAN
Sponge:	**Sponge:**
4 eggs	4 eggs
100 g/4 oz sugar	½ cup sugar
75 g/3 oz unsalted butter, melted	⅓ cup unsalted melted butter
75 g/3 oz plain flour	¾ cup all-purpose flour
Filling:	**Filling:**
150 ml/¼ pint double cream, whipped	⅔ cup heavy cream, whipped
225 g/8 oz fresh strawberries, hulled	1½ cups strawberries

Decoration:
300 ml/½ pint double cream
75 g/3 oz walnuts, finely chopped
5 strawberries

Decoration:
1¼ cups heavy cream
¾ cup finely chopped walnuts
5 strawberries

Line the bottom of two 20 cm/8 inch sandwich tins (layer pans) with greaseproof (waxed) paper and brush with oil.

Place the eggs and sugar in a heatproof bowl over a pan of hot water and whisk until thick and pale in colour. Remove from the heat and continue whisking until cool. Fold in half the melted butter and sifted flour with a metal spoon, mixing well, then fold in the remainder. Pour into the prepared tins (pans).

Cook in a preheated moderate oven (180°C/350°F, Gas Mark 4) for 25 to 30 minutes or until well risen and the sponge is shrinking from the sides. Cool on a wire rack.

Place the whipped cream for the filling in a bowl. Chop the strawberries and fold into the cream. Use the mixture to sandwich the cakes together.

Whip the cream for the decoration until stiff. Place a little in a piping (pastry) bag fitted with a star nozzle. Spread remaining cream over the top and sides of the cake. Coat the sides with the walnuts and pipe rosettes of cream around the top edge. Place a whole strawberry in the centre. Cut the other strawberries in half and place between the cream rosettes. Serve slightly chilled.
Cooking time: 25 to 30 minutes
Serves 8

Chocolate Roulade

METRIC/IMPERIAL	AMERICAN
4 eggs, separated	*4 eggs, separated*
175 g/6 oz caster sugar	*¾ cup sugar*
40 g/1½ oz cocoa icing sugar	*⅓ cup unsweetened cocoa confectioners' sugar*
300 ml/½ pint double cream	*1¼ cups heavy cream*

Line a Swiss roll tin (jelly roll pan) with greaseproof (waxed) paper and brush with oil.

Whisk the egg whites until stiff and place to one side. Working quickly, place the egg yolks in a large bowl and whisk until foamy and pale yellow, then add the sugar and continue to whisk until the mixture is thick and leaves a trail when the whisk is lifted out.

Sift the cocoa onto the egg mixture and fold in evenly with the egg whites. Pour the mixture into the prepared tin (pan) and level the top. Cook in a preheated moderate oven (180°C/350°F, Gas Mark 4) for 25 to 30 minutes or until firm to the touch.

Allow the cake to cool in the tin (pan) for 5 minutes, then invert onto a wire rack. Peel off the paper and cover with a damp tea towel or cling film (plastic wrap). Leave for at least 1 hour before filling.

Add icing (confectioners') sugar to the cream to taste, then whip until thick. Place the cake on a baking sheet and spread with the cream, then roll up like a Swiss (jelly) roll. (Invariably the cake will crack when rolled but this is quite acceptable.) Transfer to a serving platter and dust heavily with icing (confectioners') sugar.
Cooking time: 25 to 30 minutes
Serves 6 to 8

Pineapple Chartreuse

METRIC/IMPERIAL	AMERICAN
1 medium pineapple	*1 medium pineapple*
600 ml/1 pint water	*2½ cups water*
175 g/6 oz granulated sugar	*¾ cup sugar*
15 g/½ oz gelatine	*1½ tablespoons unflavored gelatin*

Using a sharp knife, remove the skin from the pineapple. Trim off the top and reserve for decoration. Remove the eyes from the pineapple. With an apple or pineapple corer, remove the hard core from the centre. Cut the fruit into thin slices.

Place the water and sugar in a pan and heat gently to dissolve the sugar, then poach the pineapple slices, a few at a time, for 3 to 5 minutes. Remove with a slotted spoon to a plate.

Sprinkle the gelatine over the syrup and stir to dissolve the gelatine, heating gently if necessary. Add any extra juice from the pineapple on the plate.

Pour a little of the jelly into an 18 cm/7 inch wetted cake tin (pan) to form a thin layer. Allow to set, then arrange the pineapple slices in even layers in the tin (pan), overlapping neatly.

Pour over the remaining jelly and leave to set in the refrigerator. Quickly dip the tin (pan) into hand-hot water and invert the chartreuse onto a platter. Decorate with the reserved pineapple top.
Cooking time: 15 minutes
Serves 6

Pavlova with Blackcurrant Sauce

METRIC/IMPERIAL	AMERICAN
3 egg whites	3 egg whites
175 g/6 oz caster sugar	¾ cup sugar
1 teaspoon cornflour	1 teaspoon cornstarch
¼ teaspoon vanilla essence	¼ teaspoon vanilla
1 teaspoon white vinegar	1 teaspoon white vinegar
Sauce:	**Sauce:**
450 g/1 lb fresh or frozen blackcurrants	4 cups fresh or frozen blackcurrants
4 tablespoons water	¼ cup water
75 g/3 oz caster sugar	⅓ cup sugar
300 ml/½ pint double cream	1¼ cups heavy cream
toasted almonds to decorate	toasted almonds for decoration

Place the egg whites in a bowl and whisk until stiff and dry. Gradually whisk in the sugar a teaspoonful at a time until half has been added.

Blend the cornflour (cornstarch), vanilla and vinegar together and whisk into the mixture with a little sugar. Gradually fold in the remaining sugar.

Line a baking sheet with non-stick (parchment) paper and spread the meringue onto the paper in a circle approximately 20 cm/8 inches in diameter and 2.5 cm/1 inch thick. Cook in a preheated cool oven (140°C/275°F, Gas Mark 1) for 1 hour. Turn off the heat and leave the meringue in the oven for another hour.

To make the sauce: remove the stalks from the blackcurrants and wash well. Place in a saucepan with the water and sugar. Heat gently and bring to the boil. Cover and simmer for 15 minutes. Cool the fruit then rub through a sieve or blend in a blender or food processor to make a purée.

Place the meringue layer on a serving platter. Whip the cream until thick and spoon into the centre. Sprinkle with toasted almonds and serve the blackcurrant sauce separately.
Cooking time: 2¼ hours
Serves 6

Five Fruit Meringue

METRIC/IMPERIAL	AMERICAN
3 egg whites	3 egg whites
175 g/6 oz caster sugar	¾ cup sugar
Filling:	**Filling:**
150 ml/¼ pint double cream	⅔ cup heavy cream
100 g/4 oz each of 5 fresh fruits, e.g. strawberries, raspberries, grapes, cherries, peaches, blackcurrants, apricots	¾ to 1 cup each of 5 fresh fruits, e.g. strawberries, raspberries, grapes, cherries, peaches, blackcurrants, apricots

Line a baking sheet with non-stick (parchment) paper and mark on a 20 cm/8 inch circle.

Whisk the egg whites until stiff and dry. Whisk in half the sugar a teaspoonful at a time. Gradually fold in the remaining sugar with a metal spoon. Spread a little meringue to cover the circle marked on the paper. Spoon the remainder into a piping (pastry) bag fitted with a large star nozzle. Pipe 5 petal shapes forming individual cases of meringue on top of the large meringue round. Cook in a preheated very cool oven (110°C/225°F, Gas Mark ¼) for 3 hours or until crisp and dry.

Carefully remove the paper and leave the meringue upside down in the oven to finish drying out as it cools.

Place the meringue on a serving platter. Whip the cream until stiff and divide between each meringue case. Prepare the fruits and fill each petal case with a different fruit, alternating colours when possible.
Cooking time: 3 hours
Serves 5

Meringues à l'Orange (page 60); Pavlova with Blackcurrant Sauce; Five Fruit Meringue (Photograph: British Sugar Bureau)

Meringues à l'Orange

METRIC/IMPERIAL	AMERICAN
3 egg whites	3 egg whites
175 g/6 oz light brown soft sugar	1 cup light brown sugar
Sauce:	**Sauce:**
175 g/6 oz orange marmalade	½ cup orange marmalade
finely grated rind and juice of 1 orange	finely grated rind and juice of 1 orange
25 g/1 oz soft brown sugar	3 tablespoons firmly packed light brown sugar
1 tablespoon rum or Grand Marnier	1 tablespoon rum or Grand Marnier
Filling:	**Filling:**
300 ml/½ pint double cream	1¼ cups heavy cream
2 teaspoons finely grated orange rind	2 teaspoons finely grated orange rind
1 tablespoon sieved icing sugar	1 tablespoon sifted confectioners' sugar
1 tablespoon rum or Grand Marnier	1 tablespoon rum or Grand Marnier

Whisk the egg whites until stiff and dry. Whisk in half the sugar a teaspoonful at a time. Gradually fold in the remainder using a metal spoon.

Line two baking sheets with non-stick (parchment) paper. Place the meringue in a piping (pastry) bag fitted with a plain nozzle. Pipe 26 to 30 medium-sized mounds onto the paper, leaving a little space between them. Cook in a preheated very cool oven (120°C/250°F, Gas Mark ½) for 1½ hours. Allow to cool and store in an airtight tin if not to be used immediately.

To make the sauce: place the marmalade, orange rind, juice, sugar and rum or Grand Marnier in a pan. Heat gently to dissolve the sugar then boil for 2 minutes until it becomes syrupy. Allow to cool.

Whip the cream until stiff and fold in the orange rind, icing (confectioners') sugar and rum or Grand Marnier. Use the cream to sandwich together the meringues. Arrange in a pyramid on a serving platter. Spoon some of the sauce over and serve the remainder separately.

Cooking time: 1 hour 35 minutes
Serves 6 to 8
Illustrated on page 59

Tarte aux Fruits

METRIC/IMPERIAL	AMERICAN
Pâte sucrée:	**Pâte sucrée:**
175 g/6 oz plain flour	1½ cups all-purpose flour
50 g/2 oz icing sugar	½ cup confectioners' sugar
75 g/3 oz butter	⅓ cup butter
3 egg yolks	3 egg yolks
2 drops vanilla essence	2 drops vanilla
Filling:	**Filling:**
150 ml/¼ pint double cream	⅔ cup heavy cream
100 g/4 oz cream cheese	½ cup cream cheese
1 tablespoon icing sugar	1 tablespoon confectioners' sugar
6 oranges	6 oranges
100 g/4 oz green grapes	1 cup green grapes
4 tablespoons clear honey	4 tablespoons honey

Sift the flour and icing (confectioners') sugar into a bowl and rub (cut) in the butter until the mixture resembles fine breadcrumbs. Bind together with the egg yolks and vanilla. Knead the mixture until smooth then chill for 20 minutes.

Place the dough on a lightly floured surface and roll out to line a 23 cm/9 inch flan tin (pie pan). Prick the bottom with a fork and line with foil. Bake "blind" in a preheated moderately hot oven (200°C/400°F, Gas Mark 6) for 15 minutes. Remove the foil and cook for a further 5 minutes. Allow to cool.

To make the filling: whip the cream until thick. Soften the cream cheese in a bowl and blend in the icing (confectioners') sugar. Fold in the cream then spread the mixture over the bottom of the flan case (pie shell).

Peel the oranges, removing all the white pith and slice into rounds. Arrange the oranges and grapes in alternate circles in the flan.

Place the honey in a pan and heat gently until bubbling and slightly thickened. Brush the honey over the fruit and leave to cool.

Cooking time: 20 to 25 minutes
Serves 6

Apricot Tart

METRIC/IMPERIAL	AMERICAN
Pâte sucrée:	**Pâte sucrée:**
225 g/8 oz plain flour	2 cups all-purpose flour
pinch of salt	pinch of salt
100 g/4 oz butter, cubed	½ cup butter, cut in cubes
50 g/2 oz caster sugar	¼ cup sugar
2 egg yolks	2 egg yolks
3 tablespoons water	3 tablespoons water
Pastry cream:	**Pastry cream:**
1 egg	1 egg
1 egg yolk	1 egg yolk
50 g/2 oz caster sugar	¼ cup sugar
50 g/2 oz plain flour	½ cup all-purpose flour
1 teaspoon vanilla essence	1 teaspoon vanilla
300 ml/½ pint milk	1¼ cups milk
Topping:	**Topping:**
350 g/12 oz fresh apricots, halved and stoned	¾ lb fresh apricots, halved and pitted
75 g/3 oz caster sugar	⅓ cup sugar
150 ml/¼ pint water	⅔ cup water
5 tablespoons apricot jam	5 tablespoons apricot jam

To make the pâte sucrée: sift the flour and salt onto a cold work surface. Make a well in the centre and add the butter, sugar, egg yolks and cold water all at once. Using your hands, gently work the mixture into a dough, drawing the ingredients together. Knead until smooth. Wrap in foil and place in refrigerator to rest.

Roll out the dough to line a 23 cm/9 inch fluted flan ring on a baking sheet. Prick base of flan and bake "blind" in a preheated moderately hot oven (190°C/375°F, Gas Mark 5) for 20 to 25 minutes. Cool on a wire rack.

To make the pastry cream: beat the egg and egg yolk together until fluffy in a heatproof bowl. Add the sugar, flour and vanilla and blend until smooth. Heat the milk until almost boiling, then pour over the egg mixture, stirring continuously. Place the bowl over a pan of simmering water and heat, stirring, until the mixture thickens. Allow to cool, then spread the mixture over the bottom of the flan.

Place the apricots in a pan with the sugar and all but 1 tablespoon water. Poach until tender. Drain and allow to cool. Arrange the fruit over the pastry cream. Place the jam and remaining tablespoon water in a pan and heat gently. Sieve (strain) and glaze the apricots. Serve cold.
Cooking time: 45 minutes to 1 hour
Serves 6

Gâteau à l'Orange

METRIC/IMPERIAL	AMERICAN
3 eggs	3 eggs
75 g/3 oz caster sugar	⅓ cup sugar
75 g/3 oz plain flour, sieved	¾ cup all-purpose flour, sifted
pinch of salt	pinch of salt
2 tablespoons orange marmalade	2 tablespoons orange marmalade
2 tablespoons Grand Marnier	2 tablespoons Grand Marnier
300 ml/½ pint double cream	1¼ cups heavy cream
2 medium oranges	2 medium oranges

Line the bottom of a 20 cm/8 inch springform tin (pan) with greaseproof (waxed) paper and brush with oil.

Place the eggs and sugar in a heatproof bowl over a pan of hot water and whisk until thick and pale in colour. Remove from the heat and continue whisking until cool. Gradually fold in the flour and salt with a metal spoon.

Pour the mixture into the prepared tin (pan) and cook in a preheated moderate oven (180°C/350°F, Gas Mark 4) for 25 to 30 minutes or until the sponge is shrinking from the sides of the tin (pan). Invert onto a wire rack and leave to cool.

Cut the cake in half horizontally and place one piece on a serving platter. Spread with the marmalade and sprinkle with 1 tablespoon of Grand Marnier. Place the other half on top and sprinkle with the remaining Grand Marnier.

Whip the cream until stiff and spread over the top and sides of the cake. Using a sharp knife, cut the rind and pith from the oranges. Cut the fruit into thin slices and arrange around the top edge of the gâteau. Serve lightly chilled.
Cooking time: 25 to 30 minutes
Serves 6

Almond Gâteau

METRIC/IMPERIAL	AMERICAN
dry breadcrumbs	dry bread crumbs
Sponge:	**Sponge:**
50 g/2 oz butter	¼ cup butter
2 eggs	2 eggs
100 g/4 oz caster sugar	½ cup sugar
100 g/4 oz self-raising flour, sifted	1 cup self-rising flour, sifted
1 tablespoon cocoa	1 tablespoon unsweetened cocoa
2 tablespoons single cream	2 tablespoons light cream
Topping:	**Topping:**
50 g/2 oz butter	¼ cup butter
50 g/2 oz caster sugar	¼ cup sugar
1 tablespoon plain flour	1 tablespoon all-purpose flour
50 g/2 oz flaked almonds	½ cup slivered almonds
2 teaspoons milk	2 teaspoons milk

Grease a 20 cm/8 inch loose-bottomed cake tin (springform pan) and coat with dry breadcrumbs.

To make the sponge: melt the butter and leave to cool. Place the eggs and sugar in a heatproof bowl over a pan of hot water. Whisk until the mixture is thick and pale in colour. Remove from the heat and continue whisking until cool. Fold in the flour and cocoa, then the melted butter and cream.

Pour into the prepared tin (pan) and cook in a preheated moderate oven (180°C/350°F, Gas Mark 4) for 30 minutes.

Have the topping ready to put on the cake. Melt the butter in a pan and stir in the sugar, flour, almonds and milk and heat, stirring continuously, for 1 minute. Slide the cake from the oven, leaving on the shelf if possible. Spread the topping over and return to the oven for a further 15 to 20 minutes or until the almonds are a rich brown and the cake is firm. Allow to cool in the tin (pan) a little before placing on a wire rack. Serve on a platter.
Cooking time: 45 to 50 minutes
Serves 6 to 8

Marron Roll

METRIC/IMPERIAL	AMERICAN
Swiss roll:	**Jelly roll:**
3 eggs	3 eggs
75 g/3 oz caster sugar	⅓ cup sugar
75 g/3 oz plain flour, sieved	¾ cup all-purpose flour, sifted
icing sugar	confectioners' sugar
Filling:	**Filling:**
1 × 250 g/8¾ oz can sweetened chestnut purée	1 × 8¾ oz can sweetened chestnut purée
6 tablespoons double cream, whipped	6 tablespoons heavy cream, whipped
Coating:	**Coating:**
3 tablespoons apricot jam	3 tablespoons apricot jam
1 tablespoon water	1 tablespoon water
175 g/6 oz chocolate, melted	6 squares (1 oz each) semi-sweet chocolate, melted

Grease and line a Swiss roll tin (jelly roll pan) with greaseproof (waxed) paper extending 2.5 cm/1 inch above the rim.

Place the eggs and sugar in a deep heatproof bowl over a pan of hot water and whisk until thick and pale in colour. Sift the flour again and fold into the mixture with a metal spoon. Pour into the prepared tin (pan) and level the top. Cook in a preheated moderately hot oven (190°C/375°F, Gas Mark 5) for 15 minutes.

Place a large piece of greaseproof (waxed) paper on a damp tea towel. Dust the paper with icing (confectioners') sugar and invert the cake onto it. Remove the lining paper and leave to cool slightly.

Blend together the chestnut purée and cream, then spread over the cake. Roll up with the aid of the tea towel.

Place the apricot jam and water in a pan and heat gently. Pass through a sieve and use to brush over the roll before spreading with the melted chocolate. Leave to set. Place on a serving platter and dust with icing (confectioners') sugar. Serve on the day it is made, cut into thick slices, with cream if liked.
Cooking time: 20 minutes
Serves 6 to 8

Index

Illustrations by Susan Neale

PDO 82-0746